I0453247

Vision Publishing House
support@vision-publishinghouse.com
www.vision-publishinghouse.com

ISBN: 979-8-9933667-2-2 (print)
LCCN: 2025922114

This book is established to provide information and inspiration to all readers. It is designed with the understanding that the author is not engaged to render any psychological, legal, or any other kind of professional advice. The content is the sole expression of the author. The author is not liable for any physical, psychological, emotional, financial, or commercial damages, including, but not limited to special, incidental, consequential, or other damages. All readers are responsible for their own choices, actions, and results.

For my mother, Theresa Sellers…

* * *

Mom, you left this world in December 2021 after a long battle with addiction, but not a day goes by that I don't feel your presence. As a kid, I never understood your in-and-outs, but I never hated you for them. I would sit and wait for your return, and when you came back, I was ecstatic, like you never left. Somehow, you always managed to bring something for me, to give me love in whatever way you could. Nothing could ever make me stop loving you.

Growing up, I realized something that shaped me deeply: it wasn't a man who first broke my heart, it was you, Mom. Your absence felt like abandonment, even though I couldn't name it at the time. I still remember the year you stole Christmas, breaking in and taking everything Granny had bought. And still, I loved you. That's the root of who I am. I learned early how to love people who hurt me.

But you were also the funnest person I knew. You lived to make people laugh, never afraid to make a fool of yourself for others' joy. I know I get that part of me from you. You always had my back. I'll never forget you hiding me and my boyfriend in the basement from Dad because you knew we weren't supposed to be down there alone. Or, the way you'd come over and clean my house better than it's ever been cleaned since.

You were my son's favorite person. He still gets sad about your absence, and I do, too. Because even though your love was inconsistent, it was still love. It shaped me. It birthed my trauma bonds, but it also taught me resilience, humor, and loyalty.

I used to blame you. But now, I understand addiction. I understand you did the best you could with what you had. And I forgive you, Mom. I would give anything for you to see me now, to see the woman I've become, the mother I am, the book I wrote. I know you'd be proud.

Your absence made me, but your love shaped me.
And both will forever live in me.

I love you, always.

Your daughter,
Tanisha

"Each time a woman stands up for herself, she stands up for all women."

— MAYA ANGELOU

Sh!t I learned

IN THE
TRENCHES

LOVE AND TRAUMA: THE SURVIVAL GUIDE FOR WOMEN WHO HAVE BEEN THROUGH IT

TANISHA WILLIAMS, LCPC

LICENSED PROFESSIONAL COUNSELOR
CEO OF THE RELATIONSHIP REHABILITATION CENTER

CONTENTS

PREFACE

My name is Tanisha Williams, a Licensed Professional Counselor from Baltimore, Maryland. With a master's degree in Marriage, Family, and Couples Counseling, I've spent years studying the battles of the heart—both in my clients' lives and in my own. This book? This is my war journal—from a soldier's account of battles fought in the trenches of love. It's a battlefield report. Every heartbreak was a combat mission, every tear a wound, and every cycle I repeated was another round in a war I didn't even know I was fighting. But the enemy was never just *them*. The enemy was my fear, my attachment wounds, and my own silence.

But hear me loud and clear: it's not just my war. If you've been through heartbreak, betrayal, or toxic cycles, then you've been drafted into this battlefield, too.

This book walks you through my personal experiences while breaking down the psychological patterns behind them. It's not just my story—it's yours, too. It's the story of anyone who has been wounded by love, anyone still carrying scars they don't know how to heal. But here's the twist: the enemy isn't just the people who hurt us—it's the fears, beliefs, and survival strategies we carry inside. This is a war against the parts of ourselves that confuse chaos for love and survival for intimacy.

This is not some self-help book filled with cookie-cutter advice about "just loving yourself" or "moving on." Nah, this is raw. This is real. This is for the ones who have cried themselves to sleep over someone who walked away. For the ones who bent over backward, hoping they'd finally be enough, just to be left questioning their worth. For the ones who keep getting up, no matter how many times love knocks them down, but are starting to wonder how much more they can take.

Every scar tells a story. But scars don't mean defeat—they mean survival. You're not weak because you've been wounded. You're a soldier who made it out of battles most people never speak about. And now it's time to stop fighting blind and start fighting with strategy.

You are not alone. And this battle? It's not over. Healing is possible, but first, you have to understand the war you've been fighting. The only way to truly heal is to face the wounds head-on, to unlearn the patterns that have been keeping you stuck, and to finally start choosing yourself.

INTRODUCTION
INTO THE BATTLEFIELD

I am not a gangster by any means. I am not a thug, but I can say I have been to war. I earned my stripes. The f^ck—I was in the mud. If you know me, you know I was in it, the thick of it. If picking the wrong one was a person, it would be me! Every time I opened my heart, the bombs flew right over Baghdad. There was always collateral damage.

Lauryn Hill said it best: *"Loving you is like a battle, and we both end up with scars."* If you've ever loved someone so deeply that losing them felt like a piece of you died, then you know exactly what I mean. Love can be beautiful, transformative, and healing; but it can also be war. And just like war, love can leave you broken, bruised, and changed in ways you never expected.

I know this because I have fought those battles. I have the scars to prove it. I have been left on the battlefield, bleeding from wounds I didn't know how to heal. So what do you do when the wounds don't close? You slap on a bandage, keep moving, and tell yourself you're fine. But that pain? It lingers. And I see it everywhere—clients, friends, strangers—walking around with unhealed wounds, struggling to understand why something meant to bring joy only brings them pain.

We've had so many negative experiences with love, and if that wasn't enough, look at how love is portrayed in the media. As a kid, I remember *The Cosby Show* and other sitcoms showing strong family dynamics, love that looked safe. Fast-forward to today—what shows promote healthy relationships? What songs celebrate real love?

Love today looks dangerous. We live in a world where everyone wants to be a savage, where vulnerability is seen as weakness, where emotional detachment is glorified. Social media has turned love into a performance, a highlight reel of relationships that often lack substance. *Love & Hip Hop* and reality TV push toxic dynamics—cheating, manipulation, emotional games—so much that dysfunction looks normal. This generation doesn't date for love; they date for what someone can offer. Love has become transactional instead of transformative.

The pressure to appear unbothered, to never "catch feelings," to move on quickly has created a generation of emotionally guarded individuals who struggle to form real connections. We operate from fear: fear of getting hurt, fear of being played, fear of looking weak. So, we armor up, put walls around our hearts, and swear we're good. But in doing that, we block the very love we're looking for.

By the time you hit your twenties, I guarantee you've felt love's sting. That sting burns like hell, and if you've been stung too many times, it's only natural to start protecting yourself. It's human nature. But at some point, you have to ask yourself: are you protecting yourself, or are you just keeping love out?

And if we're keeping it real? Most of us have built entire identities around our pain. We say we're "good" on love, that we don't need anybody, that we'd rather be alone—but deep down, we crave connection. We crave safety. We crave a love that won't leave us fighting for our place in someone's life. But when love has only ever come with pain, how do you stop running from it?

This book is for the women who've been through it and are ready to heal.

* * *

TRENCH LESSON

Lesson Learned:

Love is not meant to feel like a battlefield. When love feels like survival, it is not love—it's unhealed wounds replaying themselves. Real love should bring peace, safety, and growth, not constant pain and war.

Reflection Questions:

- What is your perception of love, and how was it shaped?
- When you think about your past relationships, do they feel more like peace or like battle?
- What is the major problem in your relationships? Has it been you or your partners?

Survival Strategy:

Begin by accessing your perception of love. Write down the first three words that come to mind when you hear "love," then reflect: are they negative or positive? If they lean toward struggle and negativity, acknowledge that as a wound—not a definition of love. Let's examine the experiences that have created these perceptions. Take each word and jot down a few experiences that reflect the word. For instance, if the word is *pain,* think of experiences that have caused you pain. These experiences represent relationship trauma. Remember these experiences.

Affirmation:

"I am worthy of a love that brings peace, not pain. I release the belief that love must be a battle in order to be real."

Your Reflection:

Alright, it's your turn. Use the space below to respond to the Trench Lesson activity and be real with yourself—no filters, no judgment.

_____

_____

_____

_____

_____

_____

_____

_____

_____

_____

_____

_____

_____

_____

_____

_____

_____

_____

_____

_____

_____

_____

_____

_____

_____

_____

_____

CHAPTER 1
THE PSYCHOLOGY OF LOVE AND TRAUMA

Every soldier is trained long before they ever see the battlefield. For us, childhood was boot camp, where we learned how to fight for love, flee from it, or surrender before the first shot was even fired. Our approach to love isn't just shaped by modern influences; it's deeply rooted in our past. Shit, it seems like even science is against us. If love is a battlefield, childhood is where we learn how to fight or how to run. This is where it all begins, where we shape our perception of love, trust, and connection. If you're dating, this should be a date-night conversation, because if you don't understand where someone came from, you won't understand how they love or why they push love away.

Attachment Theory, developed by John Bowlby, states that we are born wired for connection, and our earliest bonds shape how we see ourselves, others, and relationships. That first relationship—between caregiver and infant—sets the foundation for how we trust, regulate emotions, and experience love. A secure caregiver provides safety and consistency, creating a "home base" where a child feels protected. That safety isn't just emotional; it's biological. Proximity to a secure attachment figure literally soothes the nervous system, reducing fear and uncertainty. The way that relationship plays out determines a person's attachment style: secure, anxious, avoidant, or disorganized. Some people don't see why childhood matters in adult relationships. But this? This is the blueprint. Attachment styles don't just predict how someone loves; they explain how they handle stress, conflict, and connection.

If you've ever been with someone who can communicate their emotions, admit when they're wrong, and apologize without turning it into a war, congratulations—you just met someone securely attached. These people grew up with stability, knowing they could count on their caregivers. They developed trust, confidence, and the ability to navigate relationships with ease. A secure person can love fully and walk away when necessary. No mind games, no dramatics. They don't need chaos to feel alive, and for some, that's exactly why dating them feels boring.

Then there are those of us with insecure attachment styles: people who struggle with self-worth and trust, people whose love patterns come with triggers, cycles, and trauma responses. If you look at the way people date today, attachment theory explains so much. That hot-and-cold energy? The pursuing-and-distancing game? Ghosting? That's attachment insecurity in real time. Some people crave connection but fear rejection (anxious attachment). Others fear connection itself and run at the first sign of intimacy (avoidant attachment). And some are a mix of both (disorganized attachment), wanting love but not knowing how to handle it when it shows up.

Many of us unconsciously reenact our childhood traumas in our relationships, seeking out dynamics that feel familiar even if they are unhealthy. If you grew up feeling abandoned, you may find yourself drawn to emotionally unavailable partners, hoping to rewrite the ending. If you were raised in a chaotic or unpredictable environment, you may associate instability with passion. We unconsciously repeat the cycles of our past, trying to "win" the love we never fully received as children. The result? We walk into relationships like soldiers entering war—defensive, prepared for battle, expecting the worst. Instead of allowing love to heal us, we let our wounds dictate our relationships, reinforcing the very pain we are trying to escape.

Attachment styles come from our first run-in with love, trust, and connection—the first time we learned what it felt like to need someone. If that bond was solid, we learned security. If it was shaky, inconsistent, or painful, we learned survival.

When that first attachment goes wrong, it doesn't just disappear; you carry that wound, even if you don't realize it. It sits in the background, shaping how you move, making you second-guess love before you even get a chance to feel it. This is where the fear starts: the fear of trusting, the fear of getting played, the fear of letting someone in just for them to walk away.

And once that fear sets in, love starts feeling less like a blessing and more like a setup. When an unhealthy attachment style collides with repeated betrayal, abandonment, or toxic relationships, it doesn't just hurt—it changes you. It rewires the brain's response to love itself.

Love—something meant to bring us closeness and connection—starts to feel more like a battlefield. We begin to fear it. And when the brain perceives something as dangerous, its job is to protect you—even if you don't consciously realize it. Your brain is working behind the scenes, activating defense mechanisms designed to keep you safe from pain, even at the cost of connection.

Let's break these attachment styles down.

1. Avoidant Attachment:
The Ghoster, the Player, the One Who Won't Commit

Ever dated someone who made you feel like you had to compete for them? Someone who seemed interested but always kept you at arm's length? Someone who refused to let you in, no matter how hard you tried? That's avoidant attachment.

Avoidants are the ones who claim they "don't do emotions," the ones who drag people along but never fully commit. They crave freedom over intimacy and space over closeness. Their childhoods usually involved rejecting, unavailable, or emotionally distant caregivers. Maybe their parents abandoned them; maybe love came with conditions. Either way, they learned early that you can't rely on people to meet your needs, so they learned to rely on themselves. Now, as adults, they see emotional closeness as a threat.

Avoidants are experts at suppressing emotions. They rarely communicate their needs, viewing vulnerability as weakness. They often juggle multiple relationships—not for love but for control. Keeping multiple people in rotation allows them to have their needs met without risking attachment. And if a relationship starts feeling too deep, they create distance. They cheat. They sabotage.

And the wild part? They still want you, but only on their terms. Because love, to them, is a power struggle, and if they let you get too close, they risk losing control.

2. Anxious Attachment:
The Clinger, the One Who Loves Too Hard, the Overthinker

Ever dated someone who calls way too much, needs constant reassurance, or accuses you of cheating just because you took too long to text back? Someone who goes all in too fast and loses themselves in the relationship? That's anxious attachment.

Anxious people didn't have stable, consistent caregivers. Their childhoods were full of uncertainty: parents who were sometimes loving, sometimes neglectful; parents who struggled with addiction, mental illness, or abusive relationships; parents who were emotionally there one day and gone the next. This inconsistency made them hyper-aware of love's instability. They learned early that love isn't guaranteed. So now, as adults, they do everything to keep it.

Anxiously attached people crave connection, but that need can turn into dependency. They struggle with low self-esteem, constant fears of abandonment, and difficulty managing stress. When they feel ignored, they panic. They might blow up your phone, demand your attention, or create drama just to feel connected. It's not manipulation; it's survival instinct. Their attachment system goes into overdrive at the slightest sign of distance.

If you've ever been with someone who picks fights just to see if you'll leave, who spirals into insecurity over the smallest things, who seems to need you in a way that feels overwhelming—that's anxious attachment in action.

3. Disorganized Attachment:
The Push-Pull, the Chaos, the Love-Me-Leave-Me Pattern

Ever loved someone who made you feel like you were on a roller coaster? Someone who said they needed you, then pushed you away the moment you got close? Someone who begged for connection one minute and sabotaged it the next? That's disorganized attachment.

Disorganized attachment is the result of trauma—especially trauma that came from the very people who were supposed to protect you. These are often people who grew up in households filled with fear, unpredictability, abuse, or neglect. Sometimes the caregiver was the source of harm; other times, they just weren't equipped to handle the chaos. Either way, the message was: "Love is dangerous. But being alone is worse."

As adults, disorganized folks carry this deep split inside: they crave closeness but also fear what comes with it. They don't know whether to run toward love or run from it, so they do both. They get anxious and avoidant at the same time. One minute they're vulnerable, the next they're shutting down. They ghost, then spiral. They test boundaries, then panic when you set them.

They don't want to lose you, but they also don't know how to trust that you'll stay. So they unconsciously create chaos to feel in control—not because they're toxic, but because their nervous system has never known safe love. Their body responds to connection like it's a threat, even when their heart says otherwise.

If you've ever been in a relationship where love felt like walking on eggshells, where every good moment was followed by confusion, distance, or drama, you've experienced disorganized attachment. It's not brokenness; it's a survival response. And it can be healed—but only with a lot of safety, consistency, and unlearning.

4. Secure Attachment:
The Anchor, the Safe Space, the One Who Knows Their Worth

Ever connected with someone who didn't make you question everything? Someone who was open, consistent, and emotionally present—without being clingy or cold? Someone who made you feel safe without needing to be saved? That's secure attachment.

People with secure attachment usually grew up with caregivers who were emotionally available more often than not. Their childhoods weren't perfect, but they had a basic sense of safety—where emotions were acknowledged, comfort was offered, and love wasn't a reward you had to earn. They learned that they could trust others and also trust themselves.

As adults, securely attached folks don't treat love like a war zone or a game of survival. They value intimacy, but they don't fear independence. They're not chasing or avoiding—they're relating. They express needs without guilt, set boundaries without punishment, and listen without getting defensive. If something feels off, they talk about it. If they're hurt, they say so without needing to explode or withdraw.

Secure attachment doesn't mean perfection. It means awareness. It means knowing your triggers without letting them run your relationships. It's the ability to be close without losing yourself and to walk away from what's not aligned without spiraling into self-doubt.

If you've ever felt grounded around someone—like you didn't have to earn love, like being yourself was enough—that's secure attachment in action. It's not loud or flashy. It's steady, mutual, and healing. The kind of connection that doesn't just feel good—it feels safe.

RTSS

Your childhood shapes your attachment, society reinforces the dangers of love, and then, on top of that, your personal experiences add more wounds. That's years of repeated emotional trauma shaping the way you move in relationships. And let's be clear—emotional trauma is still trauma. That kind of pain doesn't just sit quietly in the background; it conditions you to associate love with suffering.

And now? What happens when someone is repeatedly exposed to trauma? They develop PTSD. So what do you think is happening to those of us who repeatedly experience emotional trauma from relationships?

So what is Relationship Traumatic Stress Syndrome (RTSS)? We talk about PTSD when we think of soldiers returning from war, victims of abuse, or survivors of life-threatening experiences. But what about the trauma caused by love? Relationship Traumatic Stress Syndrome (RTSS) isn't just heartbreak—it's a war on your mind, your body, and your soul. It's what happens when love stops feeling safe and starts feeling like survival.

RTSS is the collection of wounds you carry from being lied to, abandoned, manipulated, or betrayed. They're the scars you don't see but feel every damn day. RTSS rewires you: it makes you question yourself, makes you anxious, makes you push love away—or chase after the very thing that's hurting you.

It's not just a bad breakup. It's trauma. And it changes everything: how you see yourself, how you trust people, how you love. Love wasn't supposed to be a battlefield, but for some of us, that's all we've ever known.

Think about it: the one feeling we are all biologically predisposed to seek—love—hurts. And if something hurts, what do you learn to do? You learn to avoid it or protect yourself from it. When you touched fire and burned your hand, your brain coded fire as dangerous, and you automatically avoided it the next time.

Now follow me: many of us have had too many hurtful experiences with love, and now, just like the way we avoid fire, we avoid love. We develop unconscious defense mechanisms to protect ourselves from love. These defense mechanisms help us "survive" love—but in reality, they don't help us survive it; they kill it.

When love has been a source of pain, we learn to protect ourselves —sometimes without even realizing it. These defense mechanisms become our armor, keeping us from getting hurt but also keeping us from experiencing real connection.

Love begins to feel like walking through a minefield, so you keep your emotions locked up and play it safe. You dodge deep connections, make excuses, and convince yourself you don't need anyone. You keep things light, casual—never too deep, never too real. It's a survival move learned from years of seeing love come with conditions or consequences.

I used to date multiple people at once, not because I wanted options, but because I was running—running from the possibility of actually feeling something, actually needing someone.

So ask yourself: are you keeping your options open, or are you just scared as hell of real connection?

Emotional Numbing

When you've been hurt too many times, the easiest way to survive is to stop feeling altogether. You shut down, build walls so high that even you forget what's behind them. Look around—how many of your peers claim they don't have feelings?

Everybody's numb, everybody's too cool to care. But we weren't born this way. We were born to feel. Somewhere along the way, we decided that feelings were dangerous, that they made us weak, so we drowned them in substances, distractions, and temporary highs. Everybody's turnt, but nobody's really living—just numbing, just running, just trying to escape.

Hyper-Independence

You tell yourself you don't need love, don't need help, don't need anybody. It's a badge of honor—until it becomes a prison. At first, it feels like freedom; nobody can hurt you if you don't need them. But after a while, that so-called freedom starts feeling more like loneliness.

And if we're being real, hyper-independence? That shit is generational. It's passed down like a survival skill, something you learn when life forces you to be your own safety net. Being the older sibling, surviving abuse or neglect, watching a single mother hold it all together—you learn early that leaning on people is a risk, and that risk is one you'd rather not take.

So you move through life with your guard up, proving to yourself and everyone else that you don't need a damn soul. But deep down, we both know that's a lie.

We begin to develop defense mechanisms to protect ourselves from the damage that comes with connecting.

Self-Sabotage

You push love away before it has a chance to leave on its own. You pick fights, create distance, or convince yourself you're better off alone. It's easier to walk away than to risk being abandoned.

If I get even a whiff of abandonment, I'm sprinting—because better to leave than to get left, right? That's what I told myself.

But here's the problem: ever heard of cognitive distortions? They're those little lies your brain tells you, twisting reality just enough to convince you that you're protecting yourself, when in reality you're sabotaging everything good before it even starts.

Like when your partner doesn't answer the phone, and instead of assuming they're busy, your mind jumps straight to "They must be cheating." So you leave first, thinking you're saving yourself from the inevitable heartbreak.

But what if they weren't cheating? What if they were in an accident, lying in a hospital bed while you convinced yourself they were betraying you? That's the trap of self-sabotage: it makes you believe the worst so you can run before you ever have to risk getting hurt.

People-Pleasing

LORDTTT. This one—another product of abandonment. When love wasn't freely given, you learned to work for it. You do too much, give too much, twist yourself into whatever shape you think will make someone stay.

You learned early that love had conditions, that being yourself wasn't enough. You had to perform, adjust, accommodate. You had to make yourself needed just to feel wanted.

And now? You're exhausted, drained, bending over backward trying to prove your worth to people who were never meant to hold that kind of power in the first place.

Perfectionism

If you can just be perfect, maybe you'll finally feel like enough. You chase validation like a drug, thinking if you just work harder, do more, become better, you'll be loved the way you've always wanted.

But here's the thing: perfectionism will have you hiding the very parts of yourself that make you real, that make you you. The parts you're scared to show? They might just be the parts that make people love you the most.

And let's not forget where this starts. Maybe it was an overly critical parent, growing up under constant judgment, or feeling like mistakes weren't an option.

So now, you hold yourself to impossible standards, thinking if you just get it right this time, maybe you'll finally feel worthy. But perfection isn't love. It's a performance. And performing is exhausting.

Projection

You assume betrayal is coming before it ever does. Your past has trained you to expect the worst, so you start looking for signs, reading between the lines, and creating problems that don't even exist. You project your wounds onto your partner, convinced they're going to hurt you just like the ones before.

You see threats where there are none, sabotaging something real before it even has a chance to grow. And let's be real—this sounds a lot like self-sabotage, right? That voice in your head telling you, "They're just like the rest"? That's not your intuition; it's your trauma speaking.

And if you don't check it, you'll keep running from people who never had any intention of hurting you in the first place.

Emotional Detachment

Yeaaa, you want to be just like Future—a savage, nonchalant master of manipulation. Untouchable. You tell yourself you don't care, you keep things surface-level, never letting anyone get too close. Vulnerability feels like a setup, so you avoid it at all costs.

I know, because I played the same game. I couldn't beat them, so I joined them. I became one of the boys, matching their mayhem and carelessness, convincing myself I was in control. Before anything got too serious, I'd go ghost—disappear. Because in my mind, love wasn't safety; it was a liability. And I wasn't about to let anyone get close enough to hurt me.

Chasing the Unavailable

You find yourself drawn to people who can't love you back, who make you work for their affection. It's familiar. It's a script you know by heart, because it's the same damn script from childhood: chasing love, chasing attention, trying to earn something that should have been freely given.

It made it easy to keep things surface-level, to pretend you didn't care, to act like it didn't matter. But the truth? It always did. And the moment you started wanting more, needing more, that's when the frustration hit. You'd get mad, resentful even—like Why won't they love me the way I love them?

But deep down, you knew the answer. You picked them because they couldn't. That's what felt safe. That's what felt normal. And breaking free from that? That's the real work.

Overanalyzing

Mannn, it's like you automatically become a lawyer reviewing a million-dollar contract, combing through every little detail with a fine-tooth comb. Every pause, every silence, every text left on read feels like a case you need to crack. You don't just notice things; you analyze them, dissect them, and filter them through your past.

And that's where it gets dangerous. When you analyze through the lens of old wounds, through the trauma-colored glasses of your history, you start mistaking your cognitive distortions for reality. Your partner doesn't answer the phone? They must be losing interest. They're acting a little different? They must be cheating.

But what if they were just having a bad day? What if the story in your head isn't the truth?

Overanalyzing doesn't just make you cautious; it convinces you that heartbreak is inevitable, so you start acting like it's already happening before it even begins.

Now, I'm sitting here reading this, realizing I do every last one of them. Every time love comes around, you can catch me with one of these defense mechanisms strapped to my chest like armor. These aren't just habits; they're survival tactics—things we learned in childhood to protect ourselves from pain. Back then, they were innocent, necessary even. They kept us safe.

But in the game of love? These behaviors don't save us; they keep us alone. These are defense mechanisms—the things we do to stay safe.

And by the time you hit your twenties, I guarantee you've felt love's sting. That sting burns like hell, and if you've been stung too many times, it's only natural to start protecting yourself. It's human nature.

But at some point, you have to ask yourself: are you protecting yourself, or are you just keeping love out?

The truth is, these defense mechanisms don't come out of nowhere —they come from somewhere. They're born out of real wounds, real losses, real battles you've already fought. And while they once kept you safe, they also left you carrying invisible scars. That's why this isn't just theory for me—it's lived experience. I don't just teach this from the perspective of a therapist; I've been in the trenches myself.

My Story: A Survivor of Love's War

I am not just a therapist writing about this from an academic perspective; I am a survivor of RTSS. I've lived it. I've felt the gut-wrenching pain of being abandoned. I've experienced the anxiety of waiting for the inevitable betrayal. I've been stuck in toxic cycles, mistaking chaos for passion. I've been the one chasing, and I've been the one running.

And through it all, I started to recognize a pattern—one that I saw not just in myself but in almost every client who walked through my door. People are hurting. People are scared of love. People are navigating relationships with the weight of past wounds pressing on them, guiding their actions in ways they don't even realize.

RTSS isn't just something I believe exists; it's something I've witnessed every single day in my personal and professional life. I've seen the attachment styles, the cognitive distortions, and the defense mechanisms run amok in relationships. Being a therapist makes this a huge problem for me, as so many clients come in with relationship issues. People are wondering why they are having such a difficult time with love and don't even realize they are protecting themselves from it.

Many of us unconsciously reenact our childhood traumas in our relationships, seeking out dynamics that feel familiar, even if they are unhealthy. If you grew up feeling abandoned, you may find yourself drawn to emotionally unavailable partners, hoping to rewrite the ending. If you were raised in a chaotic or unpredictable environment, you may associate instability with passion.

We unconsciously repeat the cycles of our past, trying to "win" the love we never fully received as children. The result? We walk into relationships like soldiers entering war—defensive, prepared for battle, expecting the worst. Instead of allowing love to heal us, we let our wounds dictate our relationships, reinforcing the very pain we are trying to escape.

This book is the beginning of unlearning those patterns—of calling out the wounds for what they are, of healing. The war isn't over, but it doesn't have to be you against love. It's time to change the game.

But before you change the game, you have to understand the hand you were dealt and the impact it has had. We discussed society's perspective of love and relationships, how our environment and family systems shape them, and how some of us are predisposed to experience difficulty. Use this chapter to gain insight into your relational dynamics.

* * *

TRENCH LESSON

Lesson Learned:

Our brains are biologically wired to keep us safe. If you have had experiences with love that have caused you pain, your brain associates that pain with love, and that can be perceived as a threat. Once anything is perceived as harmful or a threat to that safety, your brain will protect you! Your brain will deploy defense mechanisms to keep you safe. They work, but they also make it harder to form true connections.

If you don't acknowledge your perception of love, attachment style, and defense mechanisms, you'll keep fighting battles instead of creating connections.

Reflection Questions:

- Do you have a fear of relationships and love? If so, why?
- Which attachment style do you identify with, and what experiences shaped it?
- What defense mechanisms do you use? Are they unconscious? Can you control them?

Survival Strategy:

Start mapping your attachment style. Let's look at how this attachment style was formed by core wounds and relationship trauma. Remember the experiences we wrote down earlier? Those experiences are known as core wounds. Our core wounds create our perceptions, whether true or false. Most of the thoughts formed by trauma are negative and are often false; these are known as stuck thoughts.

Look at those experiences and think about this: *What does this experience make you believe about yourself, others, or the world?* For instance, if the experience was your dad leaving, it may make you believe you are unworthy. The stuck thought is *I am unworthy.* Do this for each of the experiences listed.

Affirmation:

"I am not my wounds. I can unlearn old patterns and create a new way to love."

Your Reflection:

Alright, it's your turn. Use the space below to respond to the Trench Lesson activity and be real with yourself—no filters, no judgment.

_____

_____

_____

_____

_____

_____

_____

_____

_____

_____

_____

_____

_____

_____

_____

_____

_____

_____

_____

_____

_____

_____

_____

_____

_____

_____

_____

_____

CHAPTER 2

MY FIRST BATTLE: THE BLUEPRINT OF LOVE AND TRAUMA

elcome to the battlefield.

W Remember when I told you that your childhood was your first war? Well, welcome to my first battle. And let me tell you, the venue was a tough one. Live from the city… Baltimore City. Home of the O's. Home of *The Wire*. Bodymore, Murderland. Home of the stop-snitching movement. A city that doesn't give you a damn thing unless you take it for yourself.

Baltimore is what you make it—or at least that's what they say. But what if you ain't got much to work with? What if the cards were stacked against you before you even knew how to play?

This was the '80s and early '90s, and Baltimore was a war zone in its own right. If you weren't there, you wouldn't get it. The kind of struggle that seeps into your bones, that shapes how you walk, talk, and survive.

The neighborhoods weren't just poor; they were forgotten. Whole blocks swallowed by decay, rowhouses with boarded-up windows like blind eyes, entire communities left to rot. Abandoned buildings weren't just abandoned—they became playgrounds for kids who had no safe place to go, makeshift homes for addicts who had nowhere else to turn. And the corner stores? The only businesses still standing, selling 40s, loosies, and lottery tickets, profiting off a people barely hanging on.

And then there were the drugs. Man, crack hit Baltimore like a hurricane, and it never really left. It ran through the streets like a second economy, a new system with its own rules—one that didn't give a damn about age, consequences, or survival rates. One hit, and good people—mothers, fathers, uncles, aunties—became ghosts right before our eyes. Eyes once full of love and life turned vacant and hollow, bodies frail from the weight of addiction.

Childhood wasn't guaranteed. You grew up fast, or you didn't grow up at all. You learned early how to read a room, spot danger, keep your head down but your ears open. Trust got people killed. So did talking too much, being too soft, being too naïve. You never knew what kind of violence was waiting around the corner, but you knew it was coming. Gunshots weren't a warning; they were punctuation. Sirens weren't emergencies; they were just background noise, another part of the city's rhythm.

But Baltimore? It was different depending on where you stood. If you had money, you saw the rich culture, the history, the arts, the home of Edgar Allan Poe, the rowhomes lined up like proud soldiers. But if you didn't have shit, you saw the pain. You saw the streets. Guess which Baltimore I knew?

I came from the pain. We lived in a rowhome on the 2300 block of Winchester Street. Addiction, violence, poverty, and loss. Some of us lived through it, some of us only survived it, but nobody made it out clean. We all carried stains.

And this was the city—the battlefield, the broken foundation—where I was supposed to learn how to love. Disadvantage #1. You remember that crack epidemic I mentioned? It tore through my family.

The Foundation of Love and Survival

Love doesn't start with romance; it starts in childhood. Before we ever say "I love you" to another person, we learn what love is supposed to feel like from the people who raise us.

Some of us learned that love was safe and secure—a place to rest and feel valued. Others, like me, learned that love was unstable: one moment warm and present, the next cold and unavailable. Love was something you had to earn, and if you didn't play your cards right, it could be taken away.

I grew up in a world where survival took priority over emotional security. My mother, Theresa "Slick 50" Sellers, was a woman battling addiction, moving between jail, sobriety, and the streets. When she was around, she was everything—funny, loving, full of life. But when she was gone, I was just another child left trying to figure out what love really meant.

My father, Benjamin "Daddy-O" Williams, never got the chance to teach me. He died of an overdose when I was one. And just like that, before I could even comprehend the concept of loss, I had already lost the first man who was supposed to love me.

Rejection and Abandonment: The First Wound

People think rejection happens when you get your heart broken by a lover, but for me, rejection started before I could even walk. My father's death was the first wound. I never got to feel the love of a father, never got to be his little girl.

I grew up wondering: if he had been there, would I have felt more secure? Would I have felt more valuable, more protected? Maybe I wouldn't have spent so much time searching for security in other people. This hole burned deep.

We all know and hear about "daddy issues." They are real. Let's talk about daddy issues. People throw the term around as a joke, but there's nothing funny about the damage an absent father leaves behind.

When your father is missing—whether physically, emotionally, or both—it creates a wound. A wound that seeps into every relationship you have, whether you realize it or not. When a father is absent, a child is left to answer the question: *Why wasn't I enough to make him stay?* And that question? It stays with you. It morphs into self-doubt, into a craving for validation, into a desperate attempt to prove your worth to people who were never meant to hold that power over you.

The absent father wound manifests in different ways. Maybe you chase emotionally unavailable partners, trying to win the love you never got. Maybe you settle for the bare minimum because deep down, you don't believe you deserve more. Or maybe you've built an entire identity around not needing anyone, convincing yourself you're better off alone.

A father's love—or lack thereof—teaches you what to expect from men. If your father was absent, inconsistent, or toxic, that becomes your blueprint for love. And without realizing it, you start recreating that same dynamic, seeking familiarity over fulfillment. You chase men who leave, who make you prove yourself, who remind you—subconsciously—of the very first man who let you down.

And let's not forget hyper-independence. Some of us took that pain and flipped it into *I don't need nobody.* We became self-sufficient to a fault. We carry everything on our backs, refusing help, rejecting love, and priding ourselves on never depending on a man. But deep down? We're tired. We're carrying wounds that were never ours to bear.

And then there was my mother. She loved me—I know she did—but addiction is a beast that takes and takes until there's nothing left. Her love was like a flickering light; sometimes shining bright, other times barely there.

Her addiction was even worse than her absence, because it led to inconsistency. That toxic push-and-pull dynamic keeps you on edge, guessing where you stand. It's that emotional roller coaster of love one day, distance the next.

If you grew up with instability in love—whether from an absent parent, an emotionally unavailable caregiver, or relationships filled with highs and lows—your brain got used to chaos. And now? That chaos feels like love.

Dopamine, the brain's pleasure chemical, plays a big role in this. When love is unpredictable, your brain starts to crave the highs—the moments of affection, passion, and validation—so much that you tolerate the lows just to get another hit. So just like that, her addiction birthed my addiction to love. I've been conditioned to crave emotional instability.

That wound runs deeper. The wound left behind when the person

who was supposed to nurture you was absent—physically, emotionally, or both. A mother is supposed to be your first home, your first safe
place.

An absent mother leaves you questioning your worth in a different
way. If a father's absence makes you ask, *Why wasn't I enough for him to
stay?*—a mother's absence makes you wonder, *Am I even lovable at all?*

When the person who brought you into this world doesn't—or
can't—give you the love you need, it creates a void that no one else can
seem to fill. This wound can show up in relationships as deep insecurity, a need for constant reassurance, or even an inability to receive
love.

Maybe you find yourself always chasing the idea of family, looking
for a mother figure in your friendships and relationships. Or maybe
you struggle with trust, finding it hard to let people in because the first
person who was supposed to love you left you questioning if love is
even real.

For some, an absent mother doesn't mean she was physically gone;
it means she was emotionally unavailable. Maybe she was there but
cold, distant, or wrapped up in her own trauma, addiction, or strug-
gles. A mother who is emotionally absent leaves a child feeling unseen,
unheard, and emotionally starved.

And the way we learn to cope with that? It follows us into adulthood. Some of us become people-pleasers, always seeking approval,
trying to earn love the way we never could as children. Others develop
avoidant attachment, convincing themselves they don't need love, that
they can take care of themselves just fine. And some swing between
the two—craving love but sabotaging it when it gets too close, because
deep down, they don't believe they deserve it.

Like many other children in the city, my parents were absent—both
of them. We already know the issues that come with missing a parent.
Imagine missing both.

I carried a lot of shame as a child about my mother and her addiction. Even though addiction surrounded me, I still didn't want it to be
me and my family. The stigma of addiction, on top of the instability,
created a nasty cocktail.

A child with both an absent mother and an absent father faces a unique and deeply complex emotional struggle. When neither parent is consistently present—whether physically, emotionally, or both—it leaves a profound void in a child's sense of self, safety, and ability to form secure attachments.

A child's primary caregivers are supposed to provide love, stability, and guidance. When one parent is absent, it's damaging. When both are gone, it can feel like an emotional freefall: no foundation, no security, no blueprint for love.

The absence of both parents often leads to deep-rooted feelings of unworthiness, rejection, and emotional neglect that echo into adulthood.

What they say I should have felt—I indeed felt. To this day, no matter what I have achieved or accomplished, there is still a small voice in my head that says I'm not worthy. It was once a very loud voice, but over the years, as I've grown, it has gotten quieter.

My Grandmother, the Protector

When she was gone, my grandmother stepped in. My sister, my aunt—they all took on roles they never asked for, raising me the best they could.

My grandmother, though… babyyyy, let me say this: she was the protective factor. She did not play about me. She made it her business to show me that I was loved and that I was her favorite. She took me everywhere she could. I'd be up at card tables until the wee hours of the morning, watching her and her friends drink and gamble. I had the filthiest mouth as a child—I could cuss real good!

She took the steps to become my legal guardian when I was in elementary school. That felt good, and it meant there shouldn't be any more uncertainty in my life. She worked hard to give me everything she could.

She, however, was a giver with a gambling habit, so we didn't have much. I can recall my grandmother letting people stay with us all my life. At one point, three families were living in our three-bedroom rowhome. So you know that left me sharing a room with my grandmother for years. And with all that sharing, in the end, my grandmother lost that house. None of the people she helped ever helped her.

I saw her help everyone. I also never saw her have a boundary. She only said no if she truly didn't have it. Despite us not having much, she would always give—but she complained in silence. She would say what she wasn't going to do, but then turn around and do it the moment someone asked.

This selfless soul was my grandmother: the life of the party and the provider. My grandmother made sure I never went without—I will give her that—but what she didn't give was affection. I didn't hear her say she loved me until I went to college. She loved me by providing acts of service. Physical touch and words of affirmation were not her thing.

This was my blueprint. She is one of the reasons I made it out with only slight bruising.

But no matter how much love they gave, there was still a hole, an emptiness that whispered, *You are not enough.* Despite all of my grandmother's attempts, I knew I was different.

I spent a lot of time with my cousins and friends. Many of these families had what I didn't: a mom. My cousins had their dad and my aunt. My mother's sister also did her best to compensate for my mother's absence. She always took me with her and her family.

I spent a lot of time with my cousins, and that was cool. It allowed me to see a two-parent household. But it also made me envious. They went to the mall to shop instead of the flea market. They went on family trips. I had a good time with them; some of my best childhood memories.

However, those moments reaffirmed the fact that I wasn't good enough. My cousins were light-skinned, and I was darker. That also led me to feel inadequate.

In my life, there were so many signs that reaffirmed my inadequacy —or were they cognitive distortions, birthed from the absence of my parents?

My childhood was filled with issues that I attributed to my inadequacy. My thoughts of myself were always low. But I did a great job at hiding it. I always knew how to hide my feelings to please the people around me.

I learned not to acknowledge my feelings. Oh, those were something else that made me feel different. As a kid, I had big emotions. I was always crying about something—until my cousins started teasing me. Then I stopped crying. I started suppressing my feelings, and I've been doing it ever since.

The only feelings I showed were happiness and withdrawal.

The people in my life were all essential. Each played a role in who I have become, giving me my first interactions with relationships.

Children don't just need to be fed and clothed; they need to feel seen, heard, and held. I learned early that love was unpredictable, that the people you needed most could disappear without warning. So, I did what a lot of kids in my position did—I became a people-pleaser.

I had a deep desire to be liked, loved, and chosen. I learned to become a shapeshifter. I could survey an environment and become whoever I felt those around me needed me to be. I was liked by everyone—except the person who mattered the most… me.

What others needed became what was most important. It was easier to make people happy. If I could just make people happy, maybe they would stay. If I could be useful, maybe I wouldn't feel so disposable. Maybe then I would feel wanted, adequate, and chosen.

The thoughts I had about myself were birthed from the hand I was dealt. In hindsight, I can acknowledge the presence of distortions. I had developed a negative attachment style, which resulted in poor relational skills and cognitive distortions that made love and relationships more difficult to obtain.

The anxious attachment style was birthed from my mother's instability. Then, repeated negative experiences and perceptions of relationships put me on the path toward maladaptive connections. The odds were stacked against me as I began to arm myself with defense mechanisms to avoid more pain.

I knew that depending on people and needing them was dangerous. So I suited up with people-pleasing, self-sabotage, projection, emotional detachment, and choosing the unavailable. With these defense mechanisms—and many more in tow—I was ready to connect. Ready to love.

Reenacting the Past in Relationships

The thing about childhood wounds is that they don't just stay in childhood. They follow you into every relationship, every friendship, every interaction.

If you weren't seen as a child, you will crave visibility in relationships. If love was inconsistent, you will seek it from people who don't know how to give it freely. It's like you're trying to relive your childhood relationships as an adult, believing you have more control and can change the outcomes.

I kept dating the same person in different costumes. Sure, they looked different and had different names, but they all did the same shit. They all had the same characteristics: unavailable and inconsistent.

Does that sound fucking familiar? Yup, just like my mom—unavailable and inconsistent.

I constantly chose relationships that gave me the chance to fight for my worth and value. To fight to be seen and chosen. But each time, I wasn't chosen, reinforcing my core belief that I wasn't loved, that I wasn't enough.

Amir Levine and Rachel Heller's book *Attached* breaks this down. An anxiously attached person like me will chase after someone who pulls away, reinforcing the fear of abandonment. Someone with an avoidant attachment style will sabotage intimacy, choosing emotional distance over potential pain. Without even realizing it, we repeat the very patterns we swore we'd escape.

I played this game too many times. Falling for people who reminded me of my mother's love—there, but not really there. Chasing after men who were emotionally unavailable, thinking if I could just love them enough, they'd stay. Repeating the same story until the distortion that I wasn't worthy became a belief. A belief reinforced by experience.

Breaking the Cycle: Choosing a New Path

Learning about RTSS and the shit that leads up to it can be scary, especially when it all sounds so familiar. Especially when you realize you're not as open to love as you thought. Especially when you realize you are heavily armored and protected by defense mechanisms that keep you safe but also keep you from real connection.

But don't be fearful—be curious.

We're going to comb through the major experiences in my life that created my perspectives and birthed my fears. The thing about trauma is that it doesn't just disappear because you recognize it. You have to do the work to heal.

Understanding my attachment style was just the beginning. Healing meant learning that I didn't have to prove my worth to be loved. It meant recognizing that my past did not have to dictate my future.

For years, I lived like I was still in the trenches—fighting for love, trying to prove my worth, repeating the same cycles. But healing showed me that love isn't supposed to feel like war. Love shouldn't be the thing that wounds you; it should be the thing that heals.

The past will always be part of my story, but it no longer defines how I love. The first battle—the war for security, for love, for belonging —is over. And this time, I'm choosing to love without fear, without proving, without chasing. This time, *I'm choosing peace.*

* * *

TRENCH LESSON

Lesson Learned:

Unhealed childhood wounds write the script for adult relationships. Until you face them, you'll keep auditioning people for roles they were never meant to play.

Reflection Questions:

- How did your childhood shape your view of love and connection?
- Do you find yourself reenacting old wounds in your relationships?
- What defense mechanisms do you rely on most when love feels unsafe?

Survival Strategy:

Begin noticing patterns. Patterns help reinforce stuck thoughts. The thought that you are unworthy is a stuck thought that can be reinforced by patterns of being abandoned. Write down the last three relationships or situationships you've been in. List the similarities. Then ask yourself: Do they reinforce stuck thoughts or contradict them?

Affirmation:

"I release the need to replay my past in love. I am worthy of healthy love, peace, and connection."

Your Reflection:

Alright, it's your turn. Use the space below to respond to the Trench Lesson activity and be real with yourself—no filters, no judgment.

_____

_____

_____

_____

_____

_____

_____

_____

_____

_____

_____

_____

_____

_____

_____

_____

_____

_____

_____

_____

_____

_____

_____

_____

_____

_____

_____

_____

CHAPTER 3
THE SIDE EFFECTS OF WAR

Every battle leaves scars, whether you can see them or not. Soldiers don't walk off the field untouched, and neither do we when it comes to love. The wounds aren't always physical, but they're just as real, carried quietly beneath the armor we wear every day.

Love is supposed to build you up, but when your foundation is shaky, it can break you instead. The way we learn to love as children directly shapes our self-esteem and relationships with others.

Rejection, abandonment, and inconsistency don't just leave emotional wounds; they reshape how we see ourselves and what we accept in relationships.

This section explores how early moments of rejection shaped my beliefs about love, the roots of codependency, and the pattern of self-sacrifice that often follows.

Moments of Rejection & Its Childhood Effects

When you realize something just ain't quite right—or simply, you just fucked up—you start to wonder: *have I always been this way?*

First, have you identified your attachment style? Have you done the reflections? If so, you'll see that it all starts at the beginning, that very first relationship.

For me, with my anxious attachment style, I had to ask myself: *When was the first time I felt not enough? When did I learn that love had to be earned? Who made me feel like I had to work for affection? When did I first fear that someone I loved would leave me—whether it was a parent, a caregiver, or even a friend?*

Anxious attachment is born out of mixed signals. One minute, love feels solid; the next, it's gone like it was never there. When your caregivers gave love on a "sometimes" basis, you learned real quick that security wasn't guaranteed.

Some days, you felt seen, held, wanted. Other days? You felt invisible. And that inconsistency? That shit sticks with you. It creates this deep, gnawing fear of being abandoned.

You start scanning for signs that love is slipping away before it even happens. A delayed text? A shift in tone? A little less affection than usual? Your brain goes into overdrive. You overanalyze, replay conversations, and convince yourself something's wrong—even when it isn't.

Validation becomes your lifeline. If someone isn't actively proving they love you, your mind starts whispering that they don't. And that's the thing with anxious attachment—it's not just about *wanting* love, it's about *needing* it to feel secure. Because when love has always felt unpredictable, you'll do whatever it takes to hold on, even if it means losing yourself in the process.

Depending on your attachment style, the questions you ask yourself are different.

For those with the avoidant attachment style, one may ask: *When was the first time I felt like I couldn't rely on anyone but myself? When did I learn that needing people was a weakness? Who made me feel like my emotions were too much or unimportant? When did I first believe that closeness was dangerous?*

Avoidants learned real quick that counting on people was a gamble they couldn't afford to take. Every time they needed someone, they were either met with silence, disappointment, or some half-ass version of love that didn't feel safe. So they stopped needing. Stopped asking. Stopped expecting.

They learned that independence wasn't just a choice—it was survival. Relying on people? That was a setup. Vulnerability? That was a liability. The only person they could trust was themselves, so they built walls, kept their feelings locked up, and mastered the art of detachment.

Love, to them, feels like a trap. The closer someone gets, the more they feel like they're losing control. So they keep relationships at a safe distance—close enough to enjoy the connection but far enough to walk away before things get too deep. Because in their world, love isn't a source of safety; it's a risk. And risks? They don't take those.

Then you have the disorganized attachment style. You may find yourself asking: *When was the first time I felt like love was dangerous? Who made me feel like love could hurt me? When did I first experience both intense closeness and deep fear in the same relationship? Who in my life was both a source of comfort and fear?*

Disorganized attachment is that "love you, but don't trust you" type shit. It comes from growing up in chaos—where the people who were supposed to love you were also the ones who hurt you, neglected you, or made you feel unsafe. Imagine needing comfort from the same hands that caused your pain. That kind of confusion rewires your entire approach to love.

You crave connection, but the moment it gets too real, you panic. One foot in, one foot out. You want closeness, but at the same time, you don't trust it. You chase love, but as soon as you get it, you start looking for an exit. It's a constant war between *please don't leave me* and *I gotta get the hell outta here before you do.*

Relationships feel like an emotional rollercoaster—highs that make you feel alive, lows that remind you why you never should've trusted in the first place. One minute, you're all in, ready to love with your whole heart. The next? You're shutting down, ghosting, or sabotaging the whole thing before it has a chance to go wrong. And the wildest part? Half the time, you don't even know you're doing it. It's just muscle memory— love feeling like a battlefield because that's all you've ever known.

You see, each situation comes with a different origin. Each attachment style gives you a lens through which you view relationships. This lens impacts your beliefs, your experiences, and your actions.

With the anxious attachment style, my lens was rooted in abandonment, inconsistency, and rejection.

Attachment styles *can* change, but let's keep it real—if your life has been a series of negative experiences, that attachment style doesn't just shift because you want it to. The more you get hurt, the more those patterns get reinforced. At some point, that shit gets hardwired.

You can become self-aware—know exactly why you move the way you do—but changing it? That's a whole different battle.

When I think about healing attachment wounds, I look at it through a trauma-focused lens. Because that's what attachment issues really are: relational trauma. They shape your beliefs about yourself, about love, about what you can and can't trust—just like trauma does.

And if we're gonna address the damage, we have to start at the source: the beliefs that pain put in your head.

In trauma therapy, we call them *stuck thoughts*. These are the lies trauma told you, the stories you keep repeating to yourself: *I'm not enough. People always leave. Love isn't safe.*

These thoughts aren't just thoughts; they shape how you move, how you love, how you let people in—or don't. And the only way to undo the damage is to call those lies out and hit them with the truth.

So no, we're not just sitting here revisiting pain like it's a damn highlight reel. Nah, silly. We're digging deeper. We're figuring out what got us fucked up and why—so we can finally rewrite the script.

With my mom in and out, I was already walking around with this unspoken truth in my head: *I'm not good enough.* That was the stuck thought. The lie that rejection planted early. It came from home, from feeling unimportant, from knowing that the person who was supposed to love me most couldn't always be there.

And then? I had to step into the social arena, where validation started coming from my peers instead.

Now don't get me wrong—this is normal. Developmental even. At a certain point, peer relationships start to matter just as much, if not

more, than family. And in that space? I thrived. I always had friends. I
could get along with anybody.

And looking back, I see exactly why—it was my attachment style
working overtime.

I knew how to play small. I was agreeable. I liked whatever everybody else liked. My ability to mirror people? Insane. I could step into
any situation and blend right in, picking up on the energy, matching it,
becoming whoever I needed to be to avoid rejection. That was my skill.
My survival tactic.

And because of it, I always had people around me. But there were a
few who saw straight through that shit. And with them? I could be me.

My first real friend, Sade, clocked it from day one. She saw how I
bit my tongue, how I held back. And when I wouldn't speak up, she'd
do it for me. She had this way of saying what I didn't have the balls to
say. And funny enough, even today, she still holds me accountable
when I start shrinking myself again.

That's the thing about attachment styles—they don't just fade away.
They shape who we are when we're not even thinking about it. They
become second nature.

Avoiding rejection was my nature. But that shit got real tricky when
boys got involved. Whew. This was rough. Because now? Now I had to
actually acknowledge my feelings. Say them out loud.

And what if they didn't feel the same way? Hell no. That felt like
setting myself up to get my feelings demolished.

But some girls? They did it with ease. They'd walk right up to a boy
and tell him how they felt—like it was nothing. And mind you, we
were still in elementary school. But even then, that shit was intense.

Sade was one of those girls. Always said what she felt. Me? Hell no.
There was no way I was telling anybody I liked them. Which meant I
damn sure wasn't telling Mosean Love—the cutest boy in school—that
I had a crush on him. Nope. Not happening.

The second I even thought about it, the first thing that popped into
my head was: *There's no way he could want me.*

And just like that, my stuck thoughts won. I didn't say shit. And
guess what? I ended up with this ugly boy. Didn't like him at all, but

he liked me, and I felt like I had to have a boyfriend. Since I was too scared to speak up, I settled.

And that? That's the sad truth about avoiding rejection. It always leads to settling. You don't speak up, you have to take whatever is left. That's the cold truth.

Over time, though, I realized: "Shit, I don't want to settle. I want what I want."

So the next year, I went for it. There was Talondo, and I loved him. He was so cool, funny, and always fresh. My friends convinced me to shoot my shot. I didn't do it immediately—it took me a while. You know I couldn't be direct; I wrote a note.

He responded that he liked another girl. I was crushed. He was super cool about it and didn't make me feel weird, but it still hurt.

This time, I couldn't say he picked her because she was light-skinned and short. He picked a tall, dark-skinned girl. That sent me deep into thought because—what was it?

This was when I started thinking about how I dressed. I realized I was broke. My shoes weren't as nice as the other girls, and my uniforms were plain as fuck from Jerry's Discount Store. So not only was I tall and dark; I was also broke.

This added another insecurity. It was in fifth grade that I became obsessed with clothing. My grandmother had no idea about fashion or style. A lot of my outfits came on the same hanger. She had me in three-piece sets! I was a long way from cool.

Elementary school was when I noticed I began lying. Lying about my feelings, acting as if nothing mattered. There was no way I was going to go out sad.

I began telling people I already had a boyfriend around my aunt's house. I couldn't be the only girl without one. I had to protect myself from the reality of my thoughts. This was the birth of my defense mechanisms.

I had to protect myself from the feelings of not being enough. I couldn't let anybody else know I wasn't good enough.

This actually helped. Looking back, I realize I always lied. It began with me lying about my actual feelings toward my mother. When kids would tease me about my mom getting high, I would lie. I would minimize her behaviors and their impact. I developed this defense mechanism to protect myself from feeling inadequate.

How Rejection Warps Your Understanding of Love

Rejection was the theme of elementary school. It didn't just hurt—it left a mark that felt like it burned through my skin. Rejection creates an emotional wound that doesn't disappear; it festers if you don't deal with it. And once that wound is there, you start guarding yourself, building walls, trying not to get hurt again.

The messed up part? That wound starts whispering lies—telling you that you're not worthy of love, that you have to earn it, that who you are will never be enough.

Once you believe that, it changes everything: the way you see yourself, the way you show up in relationships, the way you believe others see you. You get critical of yourself, picking apart your flaws like everyone else is doing the same. You think if you just fix this or change that, maybe you'll be lovable.

You internalize rejection, making it feel like proof that something's wrong with you. And so, you start chasing validation and approval, trying to prove your worth in relationships—bending over backward just to feel chosen.

Rejection doesn't just hurt; it rewires how you think, planting seeds of beliefs that shape your entire life. They sound like truth because they formed during moments that felt real. You begin to think you're not enough, that your true self isn't enough. So, you shrink, overcompensate, and try to be who others want instead of who you are.

Eventually, you start believing love has to be earned, like it's something you have to prove you're worthy of. You overgive, overextend, and overfunction, hoping someone will choose you and stay. But even if they do, you don't trust it. A belief creeps in: *if you show the real you, you'll be rejected again.*

So, you wear a mask, mirror others, become who they need you to be. Vulnerability feels like a setup. And because you don't trust people to stay, you either cling too tight or push them away before they can leave. Hypervigilance becomes your norm—always scanning for rejection, convinced it's coming.

Underneath all that, there's a quiet thought that something's wrong with you. That you're broken, too much, or not enough. You start thinking maybe the rejection was deserved, that maybe you really are unlovable. And that becomes the lens through which you see yourself and others.

Rejection builds a belief system rooted in fear and shame. If you don't challenge these beliefs, they'll keep running your life.

Healing begins when you stop accepting these thoughts as facts. When you pause and ask: *Where did I learn this? Is it even true?* Most of the time, the answer is no. But you have to dig to find the truth.

Let's talk about how these deep-ass beliefs we formed from rejection don't just stay in childhood—they pack their bags and follow us right into adulthood, showing up like uninvited guests at every damn relationship we try to build.

You ever notice how you keep attracting emotionally unavailable people? Yeah, that's not a coincidence. It's familiar. It mirrors what you learned early on—that love is inconsistent, distant, or something you had to chase. So now, when someone is emotionally present and healthy, it feels foreign. Boring, even. But that person who's hot one day and cold the next? That feels like home. That feels like love, because it matches your early wounds.

Then there's the breadcrumb bullshit. You start tolerating the bare minimum because part of you believes that's all you're worthy of. A dry-ass "wyd" text at 11PM? You light up. A half-assed date where they barely ask about you? You rationalize it—*at least they made time.* But deep down? You're starving, and you're trying to survive off crumbs, acting like it's a damn meal.

And let's not even get into how your self-worth gets tied up in relationships. When you're alone, you start spiraling. *Who am I without someone choosing me?* You don't feel whole unless someone is affirming you, complimenting you, making you feel seen. That internal validation meter is broken, so you keep looking outside yourself to feel good enough.

These beliefs don't just live in your head; they live in your habits, your patterns, your choices. And until you name them, challenge them, and do the healing work, they'll keep running the show. And baby— they are messy.

Rejection and the seeds it sows are just the beginning. RTSS is built over time: repetitive experiences reinforcing our darkest thoughts.

The Early Signs of Codependency & External Validation

Let's be real—when we talk about codependency, we ain't talkin' about just "being nice" or "caring too much." Nah. We're talking about losing yourself in other people.

Like, who are you outside of them? Do you even know? Or do you shapeshift so hard to keep the peace that you forget your own needs even exist?

Codependency is when your self-worth gets wrapped up in how much you're needed. You start mistaking being needed for being loved. So you overextend. You become the fixer, the therapist, the emotional mule. You take on everyone's shit, thinking it makes you valuable.

You make yourself small so they can feel big. You become addicted to that "thank you" or *"I don't know what I'd do without you"*—even if you're silently drowning.

And then there's the whole validation thing. You're not just looking for love; you're looking for a mirror to reflect back that you're enough. If they're happy, then maybe—just maybe—you're worthy.

You ignore your own pain, your own exhaustion, your own needs, just to keep the vibe smooth. You self-abandon on autopilot.

And that's the thing—codependency doesn't look like weakness. It looks like strength at first. Like "ride or die." Like loyalty. But baby, when you're the only one riding, and you're the only one dying inside? That ain't love. That's survival. And it starts young—when love felt conditional, when being needed was the only way to feel seen.

How It Starts

Let's talk about the blueprint, because codependency don't just pop up outta nowhere. It starts in childhood, in the places where love came with terms and conditions. Where you had to *do* something to be seen.

Be quiet. Be helpful. Be strong. Be whatever made the grown-ups more comfortable. And that's when you learn: love is earned, not given.

When you have parents who are preoccupied and you come last, you learn to fight for attention. You learn to watch, to anticipate every-one's needs. You become the little emotional EMT—running around trying to fix everybody's moods before they explode.

If mom was sad, you made her laugh. If dad was angry, you tiptoed. You learned real quick that your needs came second— or not at all.

My granny wasn't hard to please—she just wanted ice and a Pepsi. I never questioned, I just did what I was told. When it came to anyone I loved, I did whatever I thought would make them happy. I would read a person, learn them, study them. Once I learned them, then I performed.

When my little sisters came over, I became a provider. I knew they were on their own in foster care, and they needed me. So whatever I had, they had.

Tweety Bird was my favorite character. Whenever my granny went out, she would buy me something. The moment my sisters came over, if they wanted it, it was theirs. And you already know my family's financial situation—it wasn't like I was being showered with gifts. I couldn't afford to give away the things I had. Once they were gone, I was left without.

Looking back, even then I kept nothing for myself. Everyone else was worthier. I felt like they needed it more.

When we become small in our lives, we learn to do things to stand out. A lot of children adopt externalizing behaviors. That child will act out in school, be the class clown, or bully others just for some attention —just for some love.

People-pleasing became your survival skill, rooted deep in that fear of abandonment. So you shapeshifted. You became whoever they needed you to be. You blended in, lost your voice, all in the name of staying close. Because the scariest thing was being left behind.

Even in early friendships, the pattern was already there. You were the one always giving—the one checking on everyone, making sure they were good, even when you weren't. You didn't ask for much. You didn't take up space. You were just happy to be included… but deep down, you were starving to be chosen.

I learned that if I did what I thought people wanted, I would be their favorite. And it definitely worked as a kid. Everyone loved me. I always got my way— *but at what cost?*

The Dopamine Hit of Validation

Why do I give everything? Because you get something from the things you do—you get credit for it. You get validation.

And validation be hittin' like a drug.

When you've been rejected enough times, approval becomes addictive. It's not just a compliment—it's a fix. It's that *"see, I am lovable"* moment that temporarily quiets all the noise in your head.

You start chasing attention like it's affection. Like if someone is watching you, texting you, choosing you… then maybe you're enough. It's easy to confuse being wanted with being valued. And that little dopamine rush you get when someone finally sees you? Whew. That shit feels like love—even when it's not.

But underneath all that is fear. The fear of being alone. Because being alone means sitting with all the lies rejection taught you—that you're not enough, not lovable, not worth the effort.

So you keep looking outside of yourself to feel whole, waiting for someone to pick you so you don't have to face that emptiness.

The Impact on Relationships

You don't just outgrow the things that kept you safe.
You carry them.
Right into your relationships.
That quiet belief that love is earned? It doesn't disappear. It just gets dressed up in grown-up behavior. Suddenly you're overgiving,

overexplaining, overapologizing—trying to prove your worth to people who should've just loved you, period.

You attract partners who take more than they give, because somewhere deep down, you believe that love is about sacrifice. You stay in toxic situations because being needed feels safer than being alone. You struggle with boundaries—saying *yes* when you're dying to say *no,* pouring from an empty cup, believing that keeping people happy will keep them from leaving.

It's not love—it's survival.

A performance.

A plea: *Don't abandon me.*

But here's the kicker: the more you self-abandon to keep love, the more invisible you become. The more you give to prove your worth, the more you attract people who are happy to let you bleed.

You become the fixer, the therapist, the ride-or-die—everything but the loved one.

And when it finally falls apart, you're left wondering why you were never enough... when the truth is, you were never supposed to lose yourself in the first place.

We make so many mistakes in love, and we have to track the origin of our issues. We confuse dysfunction for love. We mistake control for connection. Healing starts when we finally realize: love doesn't require us to shrink, sacrifice, or suffer.

Patterns of Self-Sacrifice in Relationships

So we learn to anticipate the needs of others, put them first, and people-please—all at the expense of what? The expense of *you.*

To meet the needs of others will cost you *you.*

But for someone who grew up in an environment where your needs were consistently overlooked, you learn to tuck them away, because you learn you don't matter. You learn that speaking up gets you labeled "too much," and asking for help makes you a burden.

So instead, you pour yourself into others. You show up for people who barely show up for you. You become the strong one, the reliable one, the one who always makes it work—even when you're falling apart inside.

It's not that you *want* to neglect yourself. It's that you've been conditioned to. Taking care of everyone else feels safer. Familiar. Necessary.

You feel guilty even thinking about putting yourself first. Somewhere along the way, love became a transaction: you give everything, and maybe they'll stay. Maybe they'll choose you.

Here are some examples of self-sacrifice in relationships:

- You're the one who always forgives, even when the apology never comes, even when the same hurt happens again and again.

- You over-give and overextend—buying, doing, fixing, showing up—because being needed makes you feel wanted. You start to confuse your usefulness with your value. And when you're not giving, you feel disposable.

- You lower your standards, not because you don't know what you deserve, but because *something* feels better than nothing. You tell yourself, *"At least they're here. At least I'm not alone."* You settle for crumbs and convince yourself it's a feast.

The Toll It Takes on Self-Esteem

At first, it looks like love. It feels like purpose. But over time, it begins to erode you.

You start to feel resentment bubbling under the surface, but you keep pushing it down because you don't know how to stop. You've wrapped so much of your identity around being the giver that the idea of doing anything else feels selfish.

You lose your voice. Your joy. Your spark.

You wake up one day and realize you don't even know who you are outside of meeting someone else's needs.

And then the breaking point hits—when the exhaustion sets in. When you realize that despite all the giving, you still feel unfulfilled. Still feel unseen. Still feel unchosen.

You've spent so much time making everyone else feel okay, but you're not okay. You're empty. Still searching for the kind of love that doesn't cost you everything you have to give. But here's the truth:

- Real love doesn't require your suffering.
- It doesn't ask you to disappear to be worthy.
- And it sure as hell doesn't require you to earn your place in someone's life by bleeding for it.

To sum it all up, this is exactly where I am today: overworked, underloved, and frozen in fear. The thought of someone coming to love me makes me want to set up booby traps, because the last time someone came to love me, they set the place on fire.

We've learned the science, and now you know a little bit about how this starts. But next, let's talk about the experiences that reinforce our negative thoughts of love.

* * *

TRENCH LESSON

Lesson Learned:

The wounds of rejection, codependency, and self-sacrifice don't just disappear with age. They grow with you, shaping how you love, how you give, and how much of yourself you're willing to lose.

Reflection Questions:

- Do you believe love has to be earned? If so, where did that belief begin?

- In what ways do you over-give, overextend, or self-abandon in relationships?

- What are your thoughts about yourself? Do you have high or low self esteem? Does it impact how you show up in relationships?

Survival Strategy:

Your perception of yourself influences how you show up in relationships. Our perceptions of ourselves are connected to the beliefs we have about ourselves. Some of our beliefs stem from the stuck thoughts we identified earlier.

If your stuck thought is "I am unworthy" I could imagine you would have low self esteem. If we have low self esteem we are less likely to communicate our needs or place necessary boundaries.

Let's further explore our perceptions of self. Take those stuck thoughts along with any other negative thoughts of self and list them. On the opposite side, write down facts that contradict them.

For instance: If the thought is "I am unworthy" then list facts that show you *are* worthy.

Affirmation:

"I do not have to bleed to be loved. Real love sees me, values me, and holds space for who I truly am."

Your Reflection:

Alright, it's your turn. Use the space below to respond to the Trench Lesson activity and be real with yourself—no filters, no judgment.

_____

_____

_____

_____

_____

_____

_____

_____

_____

_____

_____

_____

_____

_____

_____

_____

_____

_____

_____

_____

_____

_____

_____

_____

_____

_____

_____

_____

_____

_____

CHAPTER 4
THE WINCHESTER BATTLE

I told you all about how I grew up, my environment, and my family. Now to me.

Every soldier has a first battle, the one that tests their armor before they even know they're at war. For me, Winchester was my first battlefield. It's where I started learning how attraction, rejection, and identity can wound you long before you ever call it love.

I was always kind and nice to everyone around me. I was a great friend. As a kid, I don't think I associated myself with the word *pretty*. Especially after my elementary school debacle. I didn't think I was ugly. People made fun of the ugly people. They didn't make fun of me, but they weren't knocking down the doors to get to me either.

I was a late bloomer at that. So skinny, tall, and dark-skinned. Those were the attributes that haunted me as a kid but that I've grown to love as an adult.

Now that elementary school was over, middle school was upon us. In elementary school, relationships were happening but they weren't really a thing. But in middle school? Baby, you needed a boyfriend.

And just like elementary school, I was not prepared. I had never tongue kissed. Most of my peers had. Most of my peers had relationships over the summer. I didn't have any of those stories to tell. To be honest, the thought of someone's tongue in my mouth disgusted me. Not only did they have hookup stories, they also had growth spurts that skipped me. They had boobs, and I was flat as the textbooks they gave us. I didn't have any ass either—just a twig. Unprepared and inexperienced, I had to get with the program. I wasn't the most popular, but I wasn't a geek either. I was in the middle, and I wanted to stay there.

There were some girls that just *had it*, and I often wished I just *had it*. But it wasn't there, so I relied on my friends. My best friend from elementary school was there. I really went through middle school unseen. Just there. And I believe this is where my imagination really started to activate. I would have crushes on people and create these elaborate storylines where we were together and they loved me. Strange, right?

You have just watched the birth of a delusional woman.

I did create a storyline in which one of the boys from the baseball team wanted to date me. One summer, all of my friends were dating boys from the baseball teams. Some of them were sooo fine. Guess which one wanted me? You guessed it. He was sooo black and his lips were pink. I hated him, but he loved me. This type of guy could ruin my social status, so I remained single rather than hook up with him.

I did have one guy that I kind of liked. I said kind of because he was cute but dirty. The gag was he said he liked me too.

Whattttt. A cute guy actually liked me too? Was I about to get my first real boyfriend? The one I had in elementary school didn't count... this was the big leagues. I told my friends I liked him, and by the end of the game, we were boyfriend and girlfriend. We would talk on the phone, he would walk me home, and we even kissed. He was doing too much though—trying to come in my house while my grandmom wasn't home. I'm not sure what he was on but nahhhh.

We were together for about two weeks before I found out about the other girls. He really started to be mean once I kept saying no. Damn. So when I say no, people get upset? To a girl that always says yes, it was showing me why I should not say no.

One day he was kissing the girl outside and my friends ran and told me. I wasn't so much upset as I was embarrassed—as he was supposed to be my boyfriend, choosing someone else over me. Damn. You see that core wound reinforced. Once again, I felt like I was discarded. And this time by a dirty boy. I felt like he chose someone else because I said no. My thoughts were crazy. I instantly began comparing myself to the girl I saw him with. She wasn't very pretty, but she had big boobs. It made me hate my underdeveloped body even more.

But back to the moment. My friends ran and got me; everyone was waiting and watching for my reaction. This was one of the first times I ignored my feelings. I couldn't let anyone know I cared. I started to make fun of him—laughing, calling him dirty, and exposing the fact he couldn't spell. I told people how he misspelled words in a love letter. By the end, we were laughing at him and no one even remembered he had just hurt my damned feelings.

That was the beginning of my PR career. I would not let someone see me hurt! Remember how my cousins made me feel about crying? Ain't no way I was ready to let somebody make me cry. I definitely cried later though. I definitely cried in the corner.

The school year was always quiet for me until 7th grade. I had a boyfriend in school. He was light-skinned. (You know what, as I am writing this I think I realized how I have come to hate light-skinned men.) He liked me and came to meeee. However, he was an angry kid. He was a bad boy, always in trouble. Once again, I said no and he left.

I know one thing: I was too scared to lose my virginity, and that's all anyone wanted. So, I got dumped once again.

DUMPED. DUMPED. DUMPED.

At this point? Leave me alone.

In middle school, these relationships shouldn't count, but they all count as experiences with rejection and abandonment. They all left because I said no, or they chose other girls.

However, those incidents had *nothing* on my last middle school fiasco. Now… this boy right here. This is when the lil' girl in my panties woke up. Chilleeeee. Girls had been having sex, but I didn't really get why until this man. He was an older boy. He was 16 and I was 12 or 13. (I'm horrible with timelines, but it happened.) The fact that he liked me and wanted me? You could not tell me nothin'gggg.

That man had me sneaking. My friends got us hooked up. We would be in the stairwell of Winchester Apts making out. One day, I got my ass whipped and punished after letting him come into my aunt's house while she was gone. Aunt Candy did not play that fast-ass female shit. She sent me right home, which was only across the street.

That did not stop nothing, cause like I said, he was older so I could go over to his house. I was going over for a lil' minute. Everything was cool... until I said no. And he got real mad, too. We made it all the way to his bedroom. I was just too scared.

He told all of my friends I was a lil' girl and broke up with me in front of everybody. I couldn't even hide the hurt. Everyone knew how much I liked him. I still played it off, still kept it G. Until I got home. I cried my ass off. This is when I found out the power of R&B. Up listening to 92.3Q Jams, LaDawn Black, crying.

The next day I came outside, walking over to my cousin's house and guess what I stumbled upon. This girl I know, coming out of my ex's house. This girl was light-skinned, long hair, and she was *going!* I instantly felt terrible. However, this is where I learned about the rebound. Hanging with my cousin, I found a new man. He played on the baseball team, so he was my age. Now this boy went to church and was a good boyfriend. I can't recall why we broke up, but we were still cool.

We used to talk all the time and my cousin still talked to his cousin until they broke up. This was one of the strangest experiences with love and relationships. My cousin started dating him and didn't tell me. He ended up telling me.

Betrayalllllll.

I was pissed, but she was really one of my only friends. We stopped talking for about a week, but I forgave her. Shit. I learned to forgive people that I thought cared about me, because I didn't feel like I had a lot of people who really liked me, so I had to keep them. I learned to befriend people even though they hurt me... Crazy, right? It's actually called Stockholm Syndrome.

Now, let's talk about Stockholm Syndrome— because sometimes, the people who hurt us the most are the ones we feel the most loyal to.

Stockholm Syndrome isn't just about hostages and criminals. It's deeper than that. It's psychological survival. It's what happens when you bond with the person who's hurting you because your nervous system is too scared to let go.

It's when the line between love and fear gets blurry. At its core, Stockholm Syndrome is a trauma response. It's the brain saying, *"If I can't escape, I better find a way to feel safe here."* So you start justifying the abuse. You make excuses. You cling to the "good moments" like they cancel out the pain. You tell yourself they didn't mean it, they're going through a lot, they love me deep down. Because to admit they're actually harming you? That means facing the grief of betrayal. That means facing the reality that the person you needed to love you... just can't. And that's too much to sit with. So you attach harder. You love deeper. You perform more.

It shows up in relationships all the time.

When you defend the person who's tearing you down.

When you feel guilty for thinking about leaving.

When you start believing the abuse is your fault.

So if you've ever found yourself stuck—loving someone who hurts you, craving the same hand that broke you—please know this: it's not because you're broken. It's because your body is trying to protect you the only way it knows how.

But what kept you safe back then might be what's keeping you stuck now. And you deserve more than survival. You deserve to feel safe *and* loved at the same time.

Middle school was rough. I don't think people understand how much those years shape you. It wasn't just awkward or uncomfortable —it was painful. Rejection wasn't a moment; it was a theme. I was the girl who went unnoticed, the one who disappeared in the back of the classroom and smiled even when it hurt.

I learned early how to hide my feelings real well—mastered it like a survival skill. Because if people didn't see me, they couldn't criticize me. And honestly, I was scared of everything. Just plain ol' scary.

I didn't talk about it much at the time. But looking back, I know exactly what it was:

I didn't feel good about myself.
I didn't think I was enough.
I didn't think I mattered.

And when you don't believe you matter, you tolerate all kinds of shit just to feel like you do. That's the real danger of low self-esteem—it doesn't just make you quiet, it makes you vulnerable. You become a magnet for people who benefit from your silence. You overlook red flags because you don't trust your gut. You stay in spaces that hurt because you're scared nothing better is coming. You let people define your worth because deep down… you're not sure you have any.

Low self-esteem makes everything about survival. You don't ask for what you need because you're scared to seem needy. You overcompensate—being the funny one, the chill one, the one who never complains—because you think love has to be earned. You start performing just to be picked, and if you're not careful, you'll confuse attention for affection, and crumbs for connection.

I look back at that little girl who was always trying to be enough, and she was never the problem. She just didn't know how worthy she already was.

When you don't see yourself clearly, you leave space for the world to hand you a distorted mirror. And baby, some people will love the version of you that stays broken—because it makes them feel whole. That's why healing self-esteem isn't just about feeling confident. It's about survival. It's about protecting your peace. It's about no longer abandoning yourself just to be chosen.

I wish this was something I had my mother to teach me, or my dad to show me. There were valuable lessons I missed due to their absence.

* * *

TRENCH LESSON

Lesson Learned:

Middle school rejection isn't "puppy love." It plants seeds of self-doubt, survival strategies, and patterns of abandonment that can follow you for decades. What feels like silly teenage drama at the time often becomes the blueprint for how you see yourself in love.

Reflection Questions:

- What early relationships or "first crush" experiences shaped the way you see yourself in love?
- Do you recognize ways you've downplayed your hurt or hidden your feelings to save face?
- Have you ever excused or defended someone who hurt you because losing them felt scarier than keeping them?

Survival Strategy:

Start rewriting the script. Journal about your earliest rejection and ask: *What lie did I believe about myself because of this moment?* Then write the truth that cancels that lie. Repeat it daily until the truth speaks louder than the old wound.

Affirmation:

"I do not have to shrink, settle, or suffer to be loved. My worth is not defined by rejection; it is defined by who I am."

Your Reflection:

Alright, it's your turn. Use the space below to respond to the Trench Lesson activity and be real with yourself—no filters, no judgment.

_____

_____

_____

_____

_____

_____

_____

_____

_____

_____

_____

_____

_____

_____

_____

_____

_____

_____

_____

_____

_____

_____

_____

_____

_____

_____

_____

_____

CHAPTER 5
SHELL SHOCKED

Every war has its aftershocks. Welcome to high school. The trenches of middle school left scars, but high school? This is where I had my growth spurt, babyyyy. This was where the shit got real.

The battles weren't loud, but they were constant, fought in whispers, hallways, elections, and my own reflection. I walked in carrying invisible wounds and trying to armor up before anyone could see them.

It was the summer of ninth grade when it happened. Coming into high school was still a bit rough. But at this point, I learned how to mirror. I didn't necessarily have the confidence, but I learned how to fake it till I made it.

I learned my strengths. I was an academic; I was liked, so I became involved in student government, serving as SGA President and Senior Class President. I was actually part of my high school's history, naming the school and being part of the first graduating class.

Self-esteem was emerging a bit as I learned who I was. But the social aspect? Baby, I still struggled due to those core fears of abandonment and rejection. I wish I didn't care. Why did it matter to me so much? I just wanted to be accepted. And shit, even running for presi-dent was about being chosen.

Remember the delusions and my use of imagination? They really became a thing in high school. I created a life and lived it. I became a great storyteller. *Smh*, I know this has to be a mental disorder. But hear me out—it was a defense mechanism.

I didn't feel good, so I created a life in which I was the winner. I had a life where I was extremely popular and always had a boyfriend. I just couldn't appear to be the loser I felt like I was. But here's the thing: I never needed to lie. I had a lot of friends, but I guess I felt like I wasn't really important in their lives.

This was also the time where I entered the party scene. My best friend was my cousin Ashley, and she was the one. She was the one that got me in! If it was up to me, I would have just been telling stories about doing the things she actually had us doing.

I had hella fun as a kid thanks to Ashley. But I can't discuss Ashley without Amber and Patricia. These were critical years. They helped me really become a girl. They taught me about earrings and doing my hair. This was my girl group!

They say self-esteem is dependent upon who you are surrounded by. This is where I began to emerge. I learned about dressing and how it can impact how you are perceived. I learned to use clothing to be seen. I was tall and had long legs. At first, I hated them—but in a skirt or some shorts, babyyyy, I loved them. I learned about femininity. Thanks, ladies.

High school dragged me for filthhhhhhhhhhhh. This was a very crit-ical time. This is a stuck point. I trauma bonded, and it took me 17 years to break. This is where that Stockholm shit becomes even more relevant.

This may be the most difficult part to tell, as you know that I have always avoided criticism by minimizing things and acting as if I didn't care. However, acting as if you don't care when you do is a trauma response. It keeps you stuck and unhealed. Minimizing your feelings is essentially ignoring yourself.

I feared abandonment. And in this chapter, and some of the ones to follow, I abandoned myself. I didn't choose me—I chose others. The whole time, I was dying to be chosen while not choosing me. The ironyyyy.

Let's get to it.

Losing My Virginity

The summer of ninth grade, I lost my virginity. Yesss, it went downnnnnn.

I was the last of my friends to lose it. Yes, I was still scared, but I couldn't keep running. Also, no one was pressuring me. I was able to decide for myself, and I think that helped. But it also helped that I met a boy.

Now this boy? I loveddddddd. He had braces. I used to want to lick them, *lls*. Like, licking them is crazy, but I felt like he really saw me.

We were cool as hell together. He always made me laugh, showed me affection and attention like I had never felt. Looking back, it was only breadcrumbs of affection and attention, but I was starving, so it was easy to get hooked.

Mr. Winchester Apts had me turned out, but it was about sex. This boy wasn't even pressed and still liked me when I told him I wasn't ready. So it was clear it had to be him. He was the one. So, I waited until I was 15 years and 9 months old. August 18, 2005.

My friends helped me pick out my outfit, and I called him and said, "I'm ready." He was at his friend's house. He came home, and I lost my virginity. Then, it began. We started going together. He was my everything. I wanted to live in his skin.

He started driving, and would pick me up from school. I didn't talk to boys at my school; they hated his ass. But just like every other love interest, betrayal and rejection surfaced. But this time, it never ended.

It was on and on. I loved the source of my pain. But I never called him that. I called him my soulmate. This man was my biggest enemy.

Let's roll the tape.

Seventeen Years

Once I dropped the draws, this ninja—like all ninjas—began ninjaing. We didn't go to the same school, so he beeeeeen running amok. Myspace was the first sign I should've seen the truth.

The crazy thing was, I always believed him—and the way he made me feel. There was no way he could be lying, because he made me feel so good. He couldn't love me and be lying. That meant everyone else was lying. Right? Or, so I thought in my mind.

Even the shit I saw with my own two eyes was a lie. (That's what I tried to convince myself of!) I was number one in his Top 8 on Myspace, and then one day I'm gone. I was replaced by another girl. He lied and said it was his friend. But, I believed him.

Fast forward—he's taking her to prom. He said his mom knew her mom and he had to take her. He went to both of *my* proms. But, I went to neither of his proms.

How come she knew his mom and I didn't? There were so many questions I never asked—not because I didn't have them, but because I was afraid of the answers.

I watched him choose girls over me, and this often destroyed me— but I never cared. It was like the moment he returned, I forgot everything he had done and only remembered how good I felt when I was with him.

So, I just blindly loved him. I overlooked the red flags. I just explained them away. I made excuses for his behavior, minimized my pain, and eventually, I became just like him. I mirrored his dysfunction, and adapted to his chaos. I lost myself in the name of maintaining a connection.

What we had wasn't love; it was a trauma bond. And baby, it was the most treacherous one known to man.

Seventeen years. On and off. Highs that felt like heaven, lows that broke me open. And I stayed. When we were apart, I couldn't wait to get back to him. I was addicted. Trauma bonds don't feel like pain at first, they feel like purpose.

See, trauma bonds are formed when you connect with someone through cycles of intensity and abuse. Pain, followed by comfort. Hurt, followed by apology. Withdrawal, followed by affection. He would hurt me and love me all in the same swoop. He knew my pain, and it helped him speak to parts of me no one else could.

Both of us didn't have a dad. Both of us had moms with drug addictions. Both of us felt rejected and abandoned, and we knew how to make each other feel like the only thing that mattered. This emotional rollercoaster was mistaken for passion. But it wasn't love; it was survival mode in disguise.

When your nervous system is used to chaos, peace feels boring. Safe feels suspicious. And somehow, the person causing the most harm becomes your anchor. You hold onto them, hoping this time will be different. That the next high will finally be the love you were waiting for.

But it never is.

The truth? That relationship wrecked me. But it also woke me the hell up. He was my catalyst. He hurt me in ways I didn't even know I could hurt. But I wouldn't have become me without that dog-ass man. I had to hit that kind of bottom to realize I was chasing the same pain I grew up in.

Same patterns. Same wounds. Different face.

That's what trauma bonds do. They trick you into believing that the pain is proof of love. That the depth of your suffering means the love is real. But love isn't supposed to feel like war. You shouldn't have to lose yourself to keep someone else.

Healing means unlearning the kind of love that trains you to suffer in silence. I wasn't there yet. High school was just the beginning, but the same story kept replaying, chapter after chapter of my life.

Idolization & Pedestals

This situation had an interesting effect. I put this man on a pedestal. I idolized him, and being with him made me feel good.

Having him choose me over and over fed my ego. He gassed me, and I gassed him right back. How I saw him was how he pretended to see me. He reflected back the version of myself I was desperate to believe in: worthy, chosen, adored.

And for a while? I thought it was real. I needed it to be real.

That illusion became home base. No matter what happened—how he rejected me, how many red flags I tripped over—I always circled back to him. Because in my head, he was my person. The place where I felt seen. The one space where I believed I was wanted, needed, chosen.

That thought? It was dangerous. Because my brain believed it. Accepted it. Stamped it as truth.

See, that's the thing about the mind—it doesn't just store memories. It stores meanings. And once your brain accepts something as a core belief, it becomes your compass. You build entire patterns, relationships, and life decisions around it.

Even if it's false. Even if it's hurting you.

My core belief? *This is love. This is what being wanted feels like.* Even if it came with chaos. Even if it left me empty. Even if I had to shrink myself just to keep it. When your brain holds on to a belief—especially one tied to survival or identity—it will fight like hell to protect it. You'll ignore facts. You'll overlook behavior. You'll rewrite history. Because if the belief breaks, your sense of self shatters with it.

So instead of letting go of the person, you let go of yourself. That's how powerful core beliefs are. They don't just sit in your mind, they run your life. And when the belief is rooted in trauma or abandonment, it doesn't feel like a thought, it feels like a truth.

So, you keep going back. You stay longer. You make peace with pain. Because somewhere along the way, your brain decided: *This is what love looks like. This is what safety feels like.*

At the time, however, I understood none of this. I just always knew that he belonged to me, and I to him.

Our connection gave me confidence.

The Persona

I now had this confidence. My body had started to fill out, and I learned the power of sex appeal. I was emerging. But the whole time, I didn't know who I was, although others saw me.

It's easy to assume that the girl who walked through the halls with her head high, long legs in a skirt, SGA President, surrounded by friends—had it all together. And in a way, that was the version of me the world saw.

But there was another version. A quieter one. A version of me that no one really knew, because I didn't let them. That girl was still that scared middle schooler deep down. The one who felt invisible. The one who internalized every rejection as confirmation that something was wrong with her. The one who believed that if she could just be perfect enough, wanted enough, chosen enough, that she would finally matter.

So, I built a version of myself that could survive. I learned to mirror, to perform, to adapt. I created a persona that looked like confidence, that looked like popularity, that looked like power.

And the crazy part? It worked.

I became the "It Girl" in a lot of ways—funny and ambitious. People gravitated toward me. I didn't have self-esteem, but I had perception. And that was enough to keep me afloat. But when the noise faded, I still felt empty.

Because what do you do when the world praises a version of you that you don't even believe in? What do you do when people say you're beautiful, and all you see are the flaws? When people say you're strong, and all you feel is scared?

That was my life.

And that disconnect? That gap between how the world saw me and how I saw myself—that's where my insecurities lived. They lived in the voice that whispered, "They don't know the real you." My insecurities weren't born in high school, but they were shaped there. Reinforced. Hidden behind lashes, lip gloss, and good grades.

I was praised for being composed, for having it all together—but inside I was still trying to outrun the lie that I wasn't enough. I had learned to hide in plain sight. And what made it harder was how often other people's love became my validation.

If a boy wanted me, then I felt beautiful. If my friends hyped me up, then I felt worthy. If a teacher believed in me, then I felt smart. But when that external validation was missing? I was back at zero.

So, I poured everything into becoming desirable. Attainable. Exceptional. I learned how to win people, but I never learned how to sit with myself and feel whole. Because truthfully, I didn't think there was anything whole to sit with.

And that right there? That's where the damage starts. When you're constantly living in contradiction—being admired, while secretly loathing yourself—your entire identity becomes a balancing act. You're performing to keep the illusion alive, while quietly believing that if people really saw you, they'd walk away.

But the truth is, I was never the problem. I was just never taught how to love the unfiltered version of me. No lashes, no likes, no boy on my arm. Just me. But no one knew her—only the girl I presented.

The Double Standard

That girl began to attract the attention of the boys at my school. I curved them because I was locked down. I was the object of desire, and the fact that I was untouchable made them want me even more.

I was gassed.

I did start to like this one boy at my school. I had a crush on him, but he had a girlfriend though. I didn't care; I didn't know that lady.

My cousin was talking to his cousin, and one day I finally left Mr. Home Base, my ex. This was my first body outside of him. Mannnn, it was terrible. I was soooo mad I caught another body.

This is where I learned the lesson: never give these niggas none. The magic ends and the chase disappears. They only want one thing.

To make matters worse, you know Home Base had an issue with it.

One day, we were on the phone—we always talked like best friends despite our relationship. We talked about the other people in our lives. This shit is a red flag now. Why did his ass feel so comfortable discussing other bitches with me? Cause he ain't care!

Ughhh, I hate hindsight. But anyway...

We're on the phone, he's telling me about the new girl he talks to. I'm like, "Oh ardd, cool." I tell him about yo, and this man flips on me. Now I'm the villain. How, bro? You caught a body, too.

Welcome to the double standard. It's cool when they do it, but it's a problem when I do it. Fuck 'em. I wish. But truthfully, I immediately felt small. I disappointed the one person I felt loved me.

He didn't want anything to do with me once he found out I was no longer his. This was the first real beef that my people-pleasing couldn't fix. I thought we were done, but somehow he made it from high school to college.

The Persona's Power

Looking back, it's wild to realize how much of myself I gave away before I even knew who I was. I strongly believe having parents would have given me a stronger sense of self.

I saw my friends with mothers—they carried the lessons their moms taught them. They always had parents who reminded them of their worth and who they were.

No one ever told me.

I didn't become confident, I became good at looking like I was. I knew how to walk into a room and play the part. I had the hair, the clothes, the humor. I had presence. But presence without peace ain't power—it's just performance. And I was performing my ass off. Because underneath all of that? I was still that scared little girl, desperate to be chosen. I didn't have self-esteem. I had coping mechanisms dressed up like charisma.

What I learned, painfully, was that people often treated me better than I treated myself. And because of that, I valued them more than I ever valued me. Their approval was my drug. Their love was my mirror. And every time they chose me, I felt worthy—for a moment.

High school became the birthplace of my persona.

I couldn't beat the boys, so I joined them. I mirrored the same toxic behavior I had once cried over. I stopped being the victim and started playing the game. But no matter how well I played it, I was still losing—because I was losing me.

That relationship? Home Base? He was the storm and the shelter. My trigger and my fix. The deepest trauma bond I've ever had. I loved the very thing that broke me. And I kept going back because my brain believed the lie. It believed he was home. That thought shaped my entire identity. I made him my person, my mirror, my measure. And in doing that, I abandoned myself.

So who had I become?

A girl who knew how to be everything for everyone… except herself.

A girl who mastered the art of being chosen, but didn't know how to choose herself.

A girl who used sex, attention, and proximity to men as proof of worth—because deep down, she still hadn't found it on her own.

I was emerging, yes—but I was emerging from a place of pain. I had the style, the story, the social circle, but not the soul connection to myself.

* * *

TRENCH LESSON

Lesson Learned:

Trauma bonds disguise themselves as love. They whisper that chaos is passion, that pain is proof, and that being chosen is the same as being valued. But when love costs your peace, your worth, and your identity —it's not love, it's survival mode.

Reflection Questions:

- Who or what have you placed on a pedestal that made you abandon yourself?
- How has external validation shaped the way you see yourself?
- Are you performing to be chosen, or learning to choose yourself?

Survival Strategy:

Start separating *attention* from *affection*. Not every "want" is rooted in real love. Practice affirming your worth without relying on someone else's approval.

Affirmation:

"I no longer confuse chaos for love. I choose me first, and in doing so, I open the door for real love to find me."

Your Reflection:

Alright, it's your turn. Use the space below to respond to the Trench Lesson activity and be real with yourself—no filters, no judgment.

_____

_____

_____

_____

_____

_____

_____

_____

_____

_____

_____

_____

_____

_____

_____

_____

_____

_____

_____

_____

_____

_____

_____

_____

_____

_____

_____

_____

CHAPTER 6
BATTLE AT VILLA JULIE

I f high school taught me how to perform love, college taught me how to survive it. Villa Julie was where I marched in thinking I was grown, but really, I was still a soldier fighting invisible wars— most of them inside myself. After my run-in with Home Base, you'd think I had learned my lesson. You'd think I'd finally walk away from what hurt and walk toward what healed. But when your heart's been trained to respond to chaos, healing feels like a foreign language. And I wasn't fluent yet.

Home Base was still active. Even as I packed up for college, he came with me—in my mind, in my heart, in the way I measured every new man against him. I wasn't free, I was functioning, and there's a difference. I wasn't in control, and the fact that Home Base was still in the picture meant another identity was emerging.

If we were still messing around while he was in relationships, that made me a side chick. How many L's was I taking behind this man? It didn't matter, because whenever he spun that bend, I thought he belonged to me.

College brought new faces, new names, new situations—but the same old core beliefs followed me like shadows I couldn't shake:

- That I wasn't enough
- That love had to be earned
- That sex equaled closeness
- That attention meant affection

But just before college officially began, a new era cracked me wide open. The summer before move-in, I found myself with a new friend group. We called ourselves the SAC girls — me, Maia, Quita, and Kelly (RIP). Maia and Quita were my day ones, both living in the cul-de-sac, and Kelly completed the squad. That summer was a whole new era. It was loud, wild, and full of drinking, smoking, partying, and stepping into our womanhood in ways that were messy, thrilling, and unapologetic.

Quita was older than the rest of us, and honestly, she was a sexual guru. She taught us a lot — about bodies, confidence, how to command a room, and how to carry ourselves like we were already grown. That summer awakened something in me. I was already becoming Shantrece — the alter ego, the defense mechanism, the bold one — but the sexual confidence hadn't kicked in yet. Not until the SAC girls.

Those girls helped shape a version of me that knew how to use sensuality as power, as performance, as survival. Looking back, we were just trying to feel grown, trying to feel in control, trying to figure out how to be women — even if we were still girls inside. They didn't create a monster, but they definitely helped awaken the fire.

So, by the time I stepped into college life, I wasn't just carrying old wounds, I was also carrying this new fire, this new protection. And with it came my next phase: learning how to weaponize control.

So, I gave my body more than I ever gave my heart. And honestly, that was intentional. My heart? That shit was fragile—bruised and locked behind the door only one person had the key to: Home Base. He was still Home Base. Still the standard. Still the ache. Everyone else just got the performance.

Promiscuity, for me, wasn't just about sex—it was about trying to feel something, anything. It was me reaching for closeness without the risk of true connection. I didn't want to be loved, because love was too dangerous, too exposing, too out of my control. But being wanted? Whew. That felt like power. That felt like control. And control was something I had never really known.

When you grow up in chaos, where rejection is familiar and abandonment is expected, control becomes a fantasy you chase with everything you have. It becomes the illusion that keeps you sane. And in college, I chased that illusion through my sexuality. If I could control how you looked at me—if I could make you want me, desire me, obsess over me—then I was safe. Then I was valuable. Then I mattered. It didn't matter that it was empty, because in those fleeting moments of attention, I wasn't invisible. I was powerful.

Control gave me structure in a life that always felt unpredictable. It gave me a false sense of agency, like I was finally the one pulling the strings. But the truth? I wasn't in control at all. I was just surviving—controlling the narrative, controlling my body, controlling who got access. Deep down, I still didn't believe anyone could really love me and stay. So I made sure no one got close enough to prove me wrong. I kept the armor on. I let people see the curated version—the sexy, confident, "got it all together" girl. But behind closed doors? I was still that little girl who didn't understand why love felt like pain and why she kept giving everything away, hoping it would finally be enough.

Control became my safety net. But it also became my prison. Because the more I clung to it, the less I allowed myself to actually feel. And baby, I learned how to be numb—you would've thought I was hard up.

The boys I messed with didn't love me—they barely saw me. Some only wanted sex. With those guys, I felt in control, because I knew what they wanted and I knew how to control them. Even if I didn't control them outright, I knew how to gain leverage. Some wanted the idea of me, not the reality. I was never really dated, never courted, never shown what love should've looked like. So I used what I call the sour lemon theory—I pretended to hate the very things I desired most. I craved love, attention, and connection, but I feared them, so I moved like I didn't need them. And when I needed to feel anything real, I'd run right back to Home Base.

Last Betrayal

After Home Base, I swore I'd never love like that again. But then came my honey—sweet, attentive, soft-spoken. He was everything I thought I deserved and, at the time, everything I thought I needed. He was a walking mirror of my anxious attachment. He came in fast, loud, intense. And I mistook it all for love.

I thought the urgency meant connection. I thought the consistency meant safety. I thought the love-bombing meant real love. We latched onto each other like two people trying to outrun their own emptiness. It felt good—until it didn't. From the moment we connected, we were inseparable. We ate together, slept together, did everything together. We were codependent.

It felt like love because we were both broken in familiar ways. He was sweet, attentive, emotionally available—or so I thought. But really, he was just as anxious and insecure as I was. That's why it worked. We didn't connect through wholeness—we connected through wounds. Through abandonment. Through fear.

We needed each other, not in a healthy way, but in that *"I don't know who I am without you"* kind of way. I mistook his intensity for intimacy, and his need for me as proof that I was valuable. We were two people clinging to each other, hoping it would save us from ourselves. And because it looked like consistency—because he showed up, called, held me close—I told myself this must be love.

But it wasn't love. It was codependency dressed up in affection. We weren't building each other up—we were holding each other hostage in a trauma loop neither of us could name at the time. Still, we believed in it. We made plans for the future. We even conceived.

Then I miscarried, and that loss changed me. I grieved in silence, holding onto the fantasy of what could've been—of us being "Michelle and Obama," like my friends used to joke. He made me feel seen in a way I hadn't felt in years. Like maybe I wasn't crazy. Like maybe this was finally what real love felt like.

But there were flags. Big, waving, bright red flags. Like the fact that his baby girl was only six months old—a flag everyone saw but me. I was too busy convincing myself I had finally been chosen.

Then one day, out of nowhere, he broke up with me over something small. Petty, even. It didn't make sense—we were good, great, I thought. What happened to the forever you sold me? The future you painted in full color? And just like that, the mask dropped.

A few days later, I found out he had gone back to his child's mother. And me? I was just the rebound. The space filler. The emotional charger while he figured his shit out. The betrayal hit deeper than heartbreak—it ripped open every wound I thought I had healed. It confirmed every lie I carried:

- You're never the one.
- You're only good in pieces.
- You're forgettable once they're done needing you.

I remember the exact moment I decided vulnerability wasn't safe. It wasn't loud. It wasn't dramatic. It was quiet—sickeningly quiet. The kind of silence that settles in your chest after someone breaks your heart in a way you didn't see coming. That was the day I gave up on softness. Because the last time I tried being vulnerable, it damn near killed me.

The villain in me was born that day. She just said, *"Bet."* And that's when I stopped trying to be chosen—and started becoming untouchable.

But even in that villain phase, I was still hurting. Still bleeding. Still trying to figure out why love kept feeling like punishment.

So yeah, that betrayal changed me. Not just because of what he did, but because it taught me that sometimes, the deepest pain doesn't come from your enemies. It comes from the ones who looked you in the eyes, held your face, kissed your scars, and still chose someone else.

And you know where I went? Right back to Home Base. That song *"Who Can I Run To"* was forever the theme. Whenever somebody hurt me, I knew exactly where to go.

The Birth of Shantrece

But something in me started to shift. This was where Shantrece emerged. When Tanisha was seen as too soft, too wounded, too naïve to protect her heart, Shantrece came to take the wheel. The warrior. The one who didn't care. The one who couldn't be hurt.

If I couldn't be chosen, I'd be the one who chose. If I couldn't be protected, I'd become the protector. I had no blueprint for what I was supposed to ask for in love. No understanding of what I deserved. All I had was my trauma, my fantasy, and my body—and I used all three to try to feel worthy.

The problem? Losing yourself doesn't happen all at once. It's slow. Subtle. Silent. One decision at a time. One red flag ignored. One part of you sacrificed to keep the connection alive. I didn't even notice it at first—how every time I chose a man who couldn't love me properly, I was choosing to abandon myself too.

Every time I gave my body but held back my heart, I reinforced the lie that I wasn't worthy of being loved fully. Every time I ignored my intuition, laughed off disrespect, or stayed silent when I wanted to scream, I was slowly erasing Tanisha.

And baby, that shit caught up to me. Mentally, I was unraveling. Anxiety became my baseline. Depression came in waves. I was either overthinking everything or numbing myself completely. There was no in-between. My coping skills were survival-based, not healing-based:

- Sex
- People-pleasing
- Dissociation
- Lying to myself
- Performing confidence instead of cultivating it
- Using attention to distract from emptiness
- Using "Shantrece" to protect Tanisha

But the problem was that Shantrece wasn't healing—she was just surviving, with sharper edges. She was the shield I wore when life got too loud and love got too painful. She was the clapback queen, the don't-fuck-with-me version. But she wasn't whole. She was just tired.

And the more I leaned into her, the further I got from the little girl inside still begging to be loved. Still aching to be seen. Still crying for someone to say, *"You matter, even when you're not performing."*

Rewired by Survival

My experiences with love didn't just shape my relationships with men —they reshaped how I saw myself. They taught me to confuse sex with intimacy, to settle for attention instead of affection, and to protect myself by pretending I didn't care.

But deep down, I cared. I always cared.

And the accumulation of these experiences? The flings, the side chick moments, the betrayals, the rebound situations, the miscarried dreams, the boys who saw my body but never saw me—they rewired me. They taught me to distrust love. They taught me to distrust myself.

And the hardest part? They made me believe that survival was strength.

But covering wounds doesn't heal them. Dressing them up in confidence, distractions, and alter egos doesn't stop the bleeding. It just delays the crash. And the truth is, I've been crashing. In silence. Behind the *"I'm good."* Behind the filtered pics and curated captions. Behind Shantrece.

But I'm not ready to write a redemption arc just yet. Because healing ain't linear.

Right now, I'm still somewhere between the girl who just wants to be loved… and the woman learning how to love herself first.

* * *

TRENCH LESSON

Lesson Learned:

College showed me that surviving isn't the same as living. Using sex, control, or an alter ego might feel like protection, but it only deepens the wounds. Real strength isn't about shutting down your softness—it's about learning how to protect it without losing yourself.

Reflection Questions:

- Have you ever confused being wanted with being valued? How did it impact your relationships?
- What defense mechanisms give you a false sense of security? Do they protect you, or do they keep you stuck?
- Who is your "Shantrece"—the mask you created that shows up to survive? And what would it look like to take that mask off?

Survival Strategy:

Start by naming the masks you wear. Write them down. Acknowledge how each one has served you, but also how each one has cost you. Then, begin practicing safe vulnerability in small doses—with a trusted friend, therapist, or even in your journal. Healing happens when you learn to express yourself without abandoning yourself in the process.

Affirmation:

"I don't have to perform to be loved. My true self is worthy of love, protection, and peace."

Your Reflection:

Alright, it's your turn. Use the space below to respond to the Trench Lesson activity and be real with yourself—no filters, no judgment.

_____

_____

_____

_____

_____

_____

_____

_____

_____

_____

_____

_____

_____

_____

_____

_____

_____

_____

_____

_____

_____

_____

_____

_____

_____

_____

_____

CHAPTER 7
BATTLE OF THE LOST SOUL

By this point, love wasn't just messy, it was war. And the craziest part? I was both the soldier and the enemy. Every day felt like a mission, but the battlefield wasn't out there—it was inside me. I wasn't fighting to win love anymore. I was fighting to survive it. To dodge it. To outsmart it before it could ambush me again.

I wasn't looking for a connection anymore. I was avoiding it. Ducking behind walls, dodging intimacy like it was gunfire—because for me, it was. Vulnerability had already betrayed me more than once. So, I stopped seeking love and started guarding myself from it—aggressively.

Every new interaction came with armor. I wasn't dating—I was dodging. I wasn't exploring—I was evading. And the more I avoided real connection, the more I tricked myself into believing I was in control. But baby, I wasn't in control—I was in chaos.

And that chaos manifested in the form of defense mechanisms that appeared to be confidence but were actually emotional survival mechanisms. Promiscuity became the first line of defense. Not because I wanted sex, but because it helped me avoid attachment. If I never talked to the same person too long, they couldn't hurt me. If I kept it light, kept it casual, stayed in control of when it ended—then I was safe.

But the truth? I was crumbling inside. I started engaging in self-injurious behaviors—not just physically, but emotionally and spiritually. I was out here breaking my own heart before anybody else could. Manipulating situations, ghosting good people, pushing away anyone who saw me too clearly.

I wasn't just avoiding love. I was self-destructing in slow motion. And it hit me one day—quiet and sharp like truth always is: *I'm not just hurt… I'm at war with myself.*

The people I was drawn to during this time were just reflections of the battle going on inside. They were chaos dressed in charm. Emotional unavailability wrapped in attention. Their dysfunction made me feel seen—not because they loved me, but because they mirrored me. Hurt people? Hurt people. And I was no exception.

Tanisha—the soft, intuitive version of me—tried to come up for air during this season. She wanted to believe again. She formed attachments. She got her hopes up. But every time she peeked through, I buried her under another mistake. Another man. Another escape route.

This is also where drug use started to sneak in. Substances became yet another defense—something to soften the edges of a life that felt too sharp to touch. The parties, pills, and the kind of nights you don't talk about in the daylight. I told myself I was just having fun, just living—but really, I was numbing.

And then came the beginning of the Side Chick Chronicles. A fantasy that gave me just enough attention to feel seen, just enough intimacy to feel wanted, and just enough distance to keep me from getting hurt—until it didn't. But we'll get there.

The Bee's Era

So…boom! I had graduated college. Kinda. My degree wasn't conferred because I failed gym. Yes, you read that right. Gym. One credit stood between me and my diploma. That one credit left me stuck

—drifting, lost, standing behind the bar at The Bees wondering how I got here.

But let me tell you something. The Bees wasn't just a job. It was a season. A wild, lawless, emotional blur of a season. This was the true beginning of my villain era.

I had already been through heartbreaks, betrayals, trauma bonds, and quiet breakdowns. So by the time I got to The Bees ? Baby, Shantrece was running the show. Tanisha had taken the back seat. I wasn't crying over these men anymore—I was becoming them. I didn't walk in with my heart open; I walked in guarded, detached, and fine as hell.

I'm not going to lie to you—I ran The Bees . I was the prettiest thing behind the bar, the mysterious one all the boys tried to figure out. When I first started, I kept to myself. But that didn't stop the attention. My homeboys would pull up, dap me up, flirt heavy, and bounce— and people noticed. I had a presence. People assumed things, created narratives. And I let them.

Why not? The mystery was part of the power. I was saying very little, but making all the noise.

And then came Light Bright. Funny as hell, persistent, charming— he cracked my shell. We started vibing. He had me out with his friends, making me laugh, making me feel chosen. But what I didn't know was that he had a girlfriend. Of course he did.

The truth slapped me when one of his homeboys pulled me aside and said, "Yo, you know he got a girl, right?" And then had the nerve to catch feelings for me too. Whewwwww.

Just like that, I was tangled in a messy-ass love triangle. Light Bright had a girl. Stink (his homeboy) had a girl. And here I was— caught between both of them. Not sleeping with Stink, but still… involved. Emotionally reckless. High off the attention. Blinded by the game. Hurt people? Hurt people. And baby, I was hurting.

But let's pause here—because this wasn't just mess. This was attachment theory in action. My anxious attachment had me craving intensity. I wanted attention like it was affection. I wanted desire because I didn't believe I was worthy of real love.

And because intimacy felt unsafe, I used promiscuity and

emotional games as a form of control. Every connection was a high-stakes transaction: give just enough to keep them close, but never enough to get hurt. Stay wanted, not vulnerable. Be seen, but never fully known.

The Bees became my stage. Shantrece was the main character. And Mello—my male alter ego, my cruddy buddy, my co-conspirator—he was my mirror. If I was a man, I would've been him. Together we were running plays, partying hard, skipping feelings, collecting numbers like trophies.

This was my party era. My don't-give-a-fuck, heavy-lashed, bottle-in-hand, heart-on-lock era. And at the time, it felt like freedom. But underneath it all, I was unraveling.

I had stopped trying to heal and started trying to win. But winning at what, exactly? Who could care less? Who could stay colder? Who could play dirtier? The real gag? Nobody wins in a game that starts from pain.

So yeah… The Bees was a time. A messy, beautiful, toxic, chaotic, transformative time. I was loud. I was seen. I was chased. But I was also lost.

Back to the plot. So I was intimate with Light Skin, but spending time with Stink. People were noticing. Word started traveling around The Bees before me and Stink had even officially started dealing with each other. And when I say dealing, I mean really dealing.

At first, we were just kicking it—cool vibe, no pressure. We had good convos, laughed a lot, shared that same hurt energy. And honestly, I felt safe around him in a way I hadn't in a while. But that didn't matter. Because perception? Perception was already doing what it does best—ruining everything before the truth even had a chance to breathe.

Whispers started flying. Sides were being taken. People who couldn't even spell "loyalty" suddenly had something to say about mine. It was drama I didn't ask for—but in a way, I invited it. Because messy attracts messy. And let's be honest—this whole triangle was sloppy from the start.

Even though I knew Light Bright had a girlfriend, he never told me, and I never said I knew. One day I was over his house and he left out. I woke up to her standing over top of me. She was fuming: *Who is she? She goes to my school! Why???* Ooops. I collected my things and got out of there.

He came to me, made amends as if they had been broken up. I just went with it, because it was already made up in my mind that since you on that, I'm going see what's up with Stink! Ain't no wayyy you gonna play me and I not get my lick back. Unhealed trauma responses.

So I played it cool but started spending less time with Light Skin and more time with Stink. Stink played it cool too, 'cause we all still hung out like me and Stink wasn't laying up. We was on like second base—something in me wouldn't let me give him none, that was too freaky for me. My moral compass worked a bit. But then that shit broke all the way and I wanted blood.

We went out one day and Light Skin's girlfriend followed us. She got out, made a scene, and we left. He came home with me—little did I know she followed him and he left my house with her. Whattttttt—you let her come to my house and then leave? Bet.

The next couple of weeks Light Skin was the joke of the job, 'cause now I was out in the open with Stink. They were friends, they weren't even talking anymore. Light Skin was telling our mutual friends he was hurt. Playing the victim—you played me first, I just got even. I didn't care how I got even, but I was doing it.

Light Bright started acting different. All that charm turned cold real quick. He stopped speaking. Started sending looks across the restaurant like I betrayed him, like he hadn't been dragging me along while loving a whole other woman. But now that his boy was getting my time, it was a problem.

Oh, now I'm the villain? The audacity was wild. But that's how it goes. Men will ghost you, gaslight you, and guilt you the moment you stop waiting in the wings.

I was wrong to choose his friend, but it was fuck him at the time. As a healed adult I can say it was wrong, but back then it all was fair in love and war. What really sent it all into chaos was when Stink and I started catching real feelings. Now he wanted to see me outside of work. Now he was showing up differently—soft, consistent, lowkey territorial.

And Light Bright? He couldn't handle that it was in his face. He might not have wanted to keep me, but he didn't want to lose me either. Especially not to his own friend.

And just like that, the triangle wasn't just messy—it was explosive. The air in that place got heavy. The tension was thick. People were talking behind my back, cracking slick jokes, switching up in my face. I couldn't clock in without feeling like I was being watched, judged, dissected.

I should have been embarrassed, but I felt like that nigga. I was telling and bragging to all my homeboys about how I was ho-handling. It was fun for me—until Karma came.

I thought I was playing the game. But the game was playing me right back. Remember how Stink had a girl too? Yeaa. When we wasn't dealing with each other, me and her went out 'cause I wanted to show her I wasn't on that. And now look—two months later, after somebody hurt me... I'm on that. She was an innocent bystander, and I definitely made amends in my life with her 'cause she ain't deserve that.

I wasn't shit, lil baby. Was eating crabs with that lady, even though I didn't want her man. At that point I knew he wanted me. So me and him started spending more time with each other. This was a direct dopamine hit—as anytime we hung out it meant he had to choose me over her.

It was amusing and it boosted my ego real bad. He was doing things for me he would never do for her. Finally, I was chosen. You see how toxic that is? I told y'all I hate hindsight.

This was where being a side chick was a real thing. Let's go ahead and talk about it.

Yes—I've been the side chick. And no, I'm not proud of it... but I'm not ashamed either. Because the girl who made that choice? She was surviving. She was seeking. She was searching for something that felt like love, even if it came wrapped in betrayal.

Let's be real. There are pros to being the side chick—and that's why so many of us stay longer than we should. You don't have to deal with all the pressure of a full relationship. You get the best version of him—the one that's escaping his real life. You get the fantasy, the highlight reel.

You get to feel chosen in secret, which sometimes feels better than being ignored in public. And for a girl who grew up starving for attention, for validation, for affection? Even a secret spotlight feels like warmth.

But that warmth is temporary. And the longer you stay in that position, the colder it gets.

Because here's the cons nobody talks about: you're never fully chosen. And the worst part? You start questioning your value in silence.

If I was really all that, wouldn't I be the one?

Why do I always feel second—even when I give so much?

Being the side chick gave me access, but it robbed me of peace. It fed my ego, but it starved my soul. I knew I deserved more, but I wasn't ready to demand it. Shit, I was scared to have it. Because part of me believed that this—this secrecy, this stolen time, this emotional scavenging—was safe.

But eventually… that illusion shatters. And shattered it did.

I spent most of my time with Stink detached, doing my own thing until my feelings got involved. Catching feelings was self-sabotage; the signs were there from the start. Stink came and went as he pleased. He would move in, move out, promise me forever, then run back to her when she gave him hell. The tug of war, the highs and the lows. I was addicted. You couldn't tell me anything. I even got a tattoo across my stomach that said, "Your love is my muse" because that's what I believed his love was—a muse. It was the kind of love that hurt somebody else for me to have it. The kind where he had to choose me. This was power! I thought that meant I had finally won.

We spent months locked in this back-and-forth pattern, me and his child's mother like two parents in a custody battle. It got so twisted that sometimes we even talked like we were working together. One day I thought it was finally over, and I had won. He moved all his stuff into my place, brought his game and everything. And you know, when they plug that game in, they feel at home. I had him living in my house, not paying a single bill. And there I was, a college graduate. He had me bagging up dimes from seven grams. Me. Terrible. But that was the life I thought I wanted. Still, God wasn't about to let that settle in my life, no matter how bad I wanted it.

One day, He said, "Time's up." I came home from work and he was gone. He left me... me! How? I had my own spot, my own car, and she had nothing but some kids. I gave him peace. I gave him help. I gave him everything. And he left! My ego was crushed I did everything and lost! Everything he said she didn't do, I did!

I was stuck and completely shattered. For the first time, I crashed out. I called nonstop, cried endlessly, went by their house, and even called her. I couldn't eat or sleep; I just cried. My mother was ready to have me committed; she was about to call the crisis hotline because I didn't want to live anymore. I couldn't understand how I lost. My mind couldn't take it. My heart couldn't take it. But looking back, I don't think it was love; it was attachment. The attention, the highs, the lows, the drama— it was familiar. It was the abandonment that hurt the most. When I really think about it, the heartbreaks that tore me up the most weren't about love, they were about my ego.

Self-Destruction

Here's the science of it: Psychologically, self-sabotage is tied to your core beliefs—the ones baked into your nervous system from early experiences. If you grew up believing you're not good enough, not worthy of love, or that people always leave, you will unconsciously act in ways that confirm those beliefs. Why? Because the brain values predictability over peace. Pain that feels familiar is safer than peace that feels foreign.

Now, layer in attachment styles, and you really start to see the pattern.

- **Anxious attachment** folks (like I used to be) fear abandonment so deeply that we cling too tightly. But the moment we feel secure, we panic and push away—because we don't trust it will last. So we create drama, test people, or chase emotionally unavailable partners. We're not trying to be toxic; we're trying to control the outcome before it controls us.

- **Avoidant attachment** folks, on the other hand, have learned that closeness = danger. So they self-sabotage by creating distance. They shut down, get cold, cheat, or disappear emotionally. Not because they don't care—but because they care too much and don't know how to tolerate vulnerability.

Either way, the result is the same: we ruin the good. We attract the familiar. We replay old wounds with new people. Because healing? Healing is unfamiliar. And the nervous system doesn't care if it's healthy—it just wants what's predictable.

That's why I kept choosing chaos. That's why I kept running back to men who triggered me, mistreated me, or made me fight for scraps. That's why I couldn't let anyone really love me. Because love—real, healthy, safe love—scared the shit out of me.

And here's the kicker: people with low self-esteem will actively sabotage things that contradict their internal narrative. If deep down, I believe I'm unworthy of love, and someone comes in loving me unconditionally? I will find a way to ruin it. Not because I don't want it—but because I don't recognize it. It doesn't match the story I've been telling myself.

So I cheat. I ghost. I start fights. I shut down. I act "unbothered" when I'm really breaking. Because somewhere in my mind, losing love on my terms is safer than risking being left again. That's what self-destruction does. It convinces you that control is more important than connection. It keeps you safe… but also keeps you stuck.

And for a long time, I was stuck. Replaying the same heartbreak with different names. Smiling in public and dying in private. Choosing dysfunction because peace felt like a setup.

But here's what I had to learn: you can't heal in the same environment—or with the same behaviors—that broke you. At some point, you have to stop making yourself bleed just because you're scared someone else will cut you first. That's the thing about self-sabotage—it gives you a false sense of control. You're not protecting yourself, you're just managing the pain.

If I ruin it, I can't be blindsided. If I pull away first, I don't have to feel rejected. Control feels like safety when you've been hurt, but really, it's just fear with a good outfit on. It keeps you from trusting, from receiving, from healing.

Back to the plot. You get it—this was my Karma. This was a taste of my own medicine. It was nasty. Our very last run-in, he moved in and said he was done with her and left without telling me. I decided to pick up and move on.

You know what that meant. It was time to move on and ummmm... we got a new bartender that wouldn't stop staring. He worshipped me. He was a MAN MAN and he showed me how to be cared for, but I was already dead inside. I couldn't acknowledge who he was—I just exploited it. He was an amazing cook and he made me feel protected, but he was too nice. So I kept creeping with Stink and him. Yup, we was working together.

But I did have a conscience. I ended up leaving the bartender alone 'cause I was using him and it wasn't cool. Then he stopped talking to me. You know I can't go to work without no action. My last stop at The Bees actually saved my life.

I caught some bodies in that building. Shame was never something that I felt—I was that guy. Smh. But I wasn't a damned man, I was a lady. Who should've never been acting that way, but who raised me? THE STREETSSS. I considered myself a real nigga and no one could tell me different.

There was one more wild thing before I started to show some maturity. It was my birthday. I left the key under the mat and whoever answered me first was going be my victim!!! It was Collin's dad who answered, further elongating my Bee's hit list.

* * *

TRENCH LESSON

Lesson Learned:

When you're at war with yourself, no amount of attention, validation, or chaos will bring peace. Self-destruction masquerades as control, but it only deepens the wounds. Healing begins when you realize survival tactics aren't the same as living, and control is not the same as love.

Reflection Questions:

- In what ways have I mistaken control for safety in my relationships?
- Do my actions reflect healing, or are they simply ways to manage pain?
- Where in my life am I still replaying old wounds with new people?

Survival Strategy:

Pause and check your patterns. Notice when you're ghosting, sabotaging, or numbing instead of being vulnerable. Ask yourself: *Am I protecting myself, or am I avoiding growth?* Replace old, destructive habits with one intentional healing practice—journaling, therapy, prayer, or meditation—that allows you to feel instead of flee.

Affirmation:

"I no longer confuse control with connection. I am worthy of peace, worthy of love, and worthy of choosing myself first."

Your Reflection:

Alright, it's your turn. Use the space below to respond to the Trench Lesson activity and be real with yourself—no filters, no judgment.

_____

_____

_____

_____

_____

_____

_____

_____

_____

_____

_____

_____

_____

_____

_____

_____

_____

_____

_____

_____

_____

_____

_____

_____

_____

_____

_____

_____

CHAPTER 8
THE LIFE RAFT

This love was pure—finally, a ceasefire in the middle of a war I didn't even realize I was still fighting. It brought me peace, consistency, and stability I hadn't known before. This love wasn't chaos dressed up as passion. It was grounding, steady, and safe. It was the kind of love that gave me purpose and meaning.

Collin became my life raft in the middle of the battlefield. He was the one force strong enough to pull me out of the trenches I had been crawling through for years. This is where I found the version of myself that would clean up all this damned mess I had made. This is where things should've come together—where the healing was supposed to click.

And in many ways, it did. Having my son was the most grounding, spiritual, and clarifying experience of my life. But before he got here, life dragged me through the trenches one more time.

When I got pregnant with Lil Collin, I thought my family was complete. I thought the baby would give us the motivation to get more out of life. Instead, the pressure came hard and fast. We were homeless for a minute—couch-hopping, living out of bags. First with my cousin. Then we found a place… but it had slumlord energy. Mold, busted pipes, just unlivable. We ended up with my best friends Maia and

Quita that summer—pregnant, broke, and in survival mode. Their lights were off. We were bathing in boiled water. And I was carrying life.

But we held it down. My friends did whatever they could to make sure I was comfortable. And that's when my hustle kicked in. I don't know what it is about becoming a mother, but something inside you activates. I knew I had to provide. I didn't have the luxury of waiting for things to get better.

But did his hustle kick in? Nah. I don't think so. He was there—physically. But emotionally? Spiritually? Present in a way that made me feel supported and seen? Nope.

And it wasn't even one big thing—it was a series of little letdowns that chipped away at the illusion.

Like my birthday that year.

I was pregnant as hell, hormonal, uncomfortable, and tired. We had a roof over our head, yeah—but not much else. No money. No gifts. No plan. And him? Empty-handed. My best friends Maia and Quita went out of their way to get me a cake and to celebrate. Them doing what they could was all I wanted, all I ever asked for.

That moment was my internal breakup. I didn't say it out loud. I still went through the motions, trying to have this "two-parent household" fantasy. But my heart had already left.

I was no longer waiting to be loved. I was preparing to choose *myself*.

Micro-Cheating & Maternity

This was where the micro-cheating started. Pregnant and all!

I had also lost my job while I was pregnant. The Bees fired me—some mess involving my sister getting into a fight. But honestly? That was divine timing. I got unemployment, and for the first time, I had space to think, to plan, to rest. It became my maternity leave and my soft reset.

Big Collin ended up losing his job, and I went back to work. I got a job at Walden University—finally using the degree that I had paid for.

While working there, I enrolled in Walden as well. Started my master's in Marriage and Family Counseling. Started building something for me and my son.

And with every new achievement, my confidence grew louder than my doubt.

Meanwhile, Collin's dad? He stayed the same. He did get back to work at another The Bees , and that came with its own drama. He was starting to talk to different girls. To be fair, he was a good father—loving, present, involved. But emotionally, he was stuck. Content. Comfortable with "just enough."

And I was no longer that girl. I wanted more—for me, for my son, for the life I was growing into. His love was… okay. But I was no longer okay with mild love.

I felt terrible, though, because I knew he loved me—but I no longer loved him. We broke up a couple of times, and this was the one time I actually used logic over emotions. I knew that I could settle and Lil Collin would be happy, his dad would be happy—but I wouldn't. Usually, that would have been enough for me, but surprisingly, it wasn't.

I felt like his dad deserved a love like the one he had given me. However, little did I know, this started Big Collin's villain era. He was quite mean after our relationship.

One day, Big Collin posted a girl. Posted a girl right after leaving my house and borrowing cigarette money. That shit sent me. I replied on the post like, "Great—come get ya stuff and live with her."

Just like that, me and him ended.

We never looked back. Today, he's actually one of my favorite people. I believe it was possible because we stopped the relationship before we started to truly hurt each other.

Choosing Me

Letting him go—despite his resistance—showed me I had grown. Normally, I would have done whatever made everyone else happy, but this time I chose me. I was proud because I finally listened to Tanisha. I realized I wasn't asking for too much—I was just asking the wrong person. This was the moment I stopped shrinking to fit into someone else's version of love.

Tanisha stood all the way up. Not Shantrece. Not the performer. Not the survivor. But the mother. The scholar. The woman. The one who finally understood that being chosen by someone else means nothing if you keep abandoning yourself. And I wasn't abandoning me ever again. (Or at least, so I thought.)

This was also a critical time because my image began to change. I started making real money. I was getting refund checks from school, investing in myself, and finally able to get bust-down weaves in the salons—no more kitchen styles. I had leveled the fuck up! On the outside, I looked like I was glowing and growing.

But in the love department? Nothing had changed. I was still guarded, still carrying the same fears, and still expecting something different while repeating the same patterns. After I left Big Collin, I can't even clearly recall what I was doing—but what I do know is that I spent my life bouncing between past flings. From Home Base, to Honey, and then onto my next toxic thing, I was still circling the same cycle.

Sneaky Links & Empty Fling Seasons

The next fling, I can't really say it was about self-esteem—but it definitely wasn't a good look. I linked up with a dude everybody knew was a slut. A slut that even knew Home Base. Did I care? Honestly, I did. But it was a sneaky link, and I thought no one would ever know… as long as he kept it P.

Things were dry at the time, but a couple years back, Mello had made a connection for me. I was home, sad on my birthday, and he was like, "Our homeboy's bday today, too—how about y'all link?" We did, and we had a time. That man became my birthday twin. For the next couple of years, we celebrated together. On our first link, he tried to hit, but there was no wayyy I was letting him crack first day. He was a known ho-handler. And if I thought I wasn't shit, he was ten times worse.

Dealing with him was just becoming another notch on the belt, but at that time, I just needed something fun—and fun, indeed, it was. He would scoop me, slide my momma some money to watch my son, and take me out. He had money, and we were always in a section having a time. But there was always some girl in the background, always some side drama. He wanted to go out all the time, but eventually, I started to hate it—especially once I gave in. Ughhhhhh, hindsight is brutal. But whatever—it happened, and we were flying under the radar. That shit was lit… until he started running his mouth.

See, I hadn't even told Mello we were creeping. One day, I was over his house, he stepped out, and suddenly my brothers were blowing up my phone. I finally answered, and Mello's like, "So it's true—you in that nigga's bed?" Man, the cover was blown. That's when the whole thing turned phony. I was cool messing with him when no one knew. But once word got out, it felt like eyes were on me every time he was with another chick or on some nut shit.

It was fun while it lasted, but short-lived—especially when Home Base found out. I don't know why I thought he wouldn't, but he was pissed. He made me feel like I was "for the streets" after being with my birthday twin. Whole time, though, he was just playing the game— dragging me for filth the whole way. The bigger picture? He still felt like I belonged to him. He wasn't ready to let me be with another man. He had to show dominance. So when he said, "Cut that man off," I did. And just like that, Home Base was back active.

The Trap of Emotionally Unavailable Men

I look at the list of bodies I caught, and there's a clear theme: emotionally unavailable men. But why? Let's talk about them—the ones who leave you guessing, who love you just enough to keep you around but never enough to make you feel secure. The ones who know how to touch your body but never your soul. The ones who say they care but never show up when it counts.

For the longest time, those were my kryptonite. I craved them. Wanted them. Felt like I needed them. And no matter how much they disappointed me, I kept going back—like clockwork.

Looking back now, I realize I was recreating my childhood stage—performing for their love and attention, feeling victorious whenever I got just a little. I remember saying I hated people who liked me, and I was only interested in guys who didn't. Because it gave me a chance to compete. A chance to win. And in my broken logic, that was love for me.

Science of the Highs & Lows

So I had to ask myself: *Why?* And the answer wasn't just emotional—it was neurological. It was science. When you grow up in environments where love is inconsistent—when the people who are supposed to love you are also the ones who hurt you—you develop what's called an insecure attachment style. Your brain wires itself to associate love with unpredictability, with tension, with chaos.

So when someone shows up half-present, when they make you work for their affection, when they breadcrumb you just enough to stay hopeful—that feels like home. It doesn't feel wrong—it feels familiar. And that's the danger. Emotionally unavailable men provided a false sense of security. Because the chase, the unpredictability, the rare, intoxicating moments when they actually did show up—that became the reward. The "high." The proof that maybe you were lovable, after all.

And that right there is the same cycle that fuels addiction. From a neurological standpoint, love—especially inconsistent love—activates the same reward system in the brain as drugs and gambling. The highs are euphoric. The dopamine rush when he finally calls, finally touches you, finally says something sweet—it's intoxicating. It's relief. It's proof that you're enough—for that moment.

But then comes the crash. The silence. The distance. The broken promise. The lie. Suddenly, you're spiraling, desperate for your next fix. So you reach out, you beg, you cry, you forgive—just to feel that high again. But scratch that last part—I learned not to do that. I learned to act like I didn't care. If I cried, it would be home alone.

And we convince ourselves that this is love. That love is supposed to be painful, inconsistent, anxiety-inducing. That if we can just work harder, love better, be more, stay longer—he'll finally see us. But baby, what you're chasing isn't love. It's a chemical loop of trauma reinforcement. And the men? They're just triggers. Mirrors of the wound. Providers of the rush.

I thought I wanted love. But I was addicted to the possibility of love. Real love scared the shit out of me—and I sabotaged it anytime I felt anything like it. Emotionally unavailable men kept me safe from love—but they damaged me in other ways. They don't offer safety—they offer survival mode. They don't offer love—they offer confusion. And they don't help you feel whole—they keep you chasing the parts of yourself you lost trying to win them over.

The Ultimate Betrayal

Somewhere in the middle of my chaos—between The Bees drama, motherhood, and trying to find myself—he started a family. Home Base. The man who had held my heart hostage for over a decade. The man I thought I'd always circle back to.

I found out at a friend's wedding. I was in a dress, drink in hand, smiling and laughing, when someone said it casually—like it wasn't going to knock the wind out of me. I looked over and saw them walk in, and her belly was huge. My chest caved. I ran out of there, couldn't breathe, because in that moment my whole body screamed, *Damn… that was supposed to be us.* Where did she even come from? How did we go from *"You're my soulmate"* to this?

This man had told me he didn't even like her. Said she was just a freak, said it didn't mean anything. But now? Y'all having a family. It felt like betrayal. But here's the twist—I didn't even feel like I had the right to be betrayed. We weren't together. I had a child too. He was just "living his life." So I did what I always did—made excuses for him, minimized my own feelings, told myself I was tripping, silenced my heartbreak like it wasn't valid.

But that pain cut deep. Because even if we weren't together, we had history. We had promises. And whether we said it out loud or not, I always thought we'd find our way back. And right when I was choking on that heartbreak, he came back—like always—with a sob story. He said his baby mother abandoned him. Said she stopped being affectionate, stopped being intimate, said she changed. And like a fool with a bleeding heart, I ran straight to him. Didn't ask questions. Didn't think. I just activated protection mode like, *"Nobody hurts my baby."*

I didn't even pause to ask, *"What did you do to her?"* Because the man who had hurt me the most could still make me feel like it was my job to rescue him. So I showed up. Played my role. No title, no clarity —just vibes and loyalty. I even pulled up to the house they shared, but he said they weren't together, just staying with her parents. And then? Boom. Another baby. Another disappearing act. Gone again.

I sat there with myself like, *How did I let this happen again?* I tried to remember what stories he told me, what lies I swallowed whole. But the truth? He never really had to lie. He never had to explain—because I never demanded it. I never held him accountable. Every time he disappeared, I'd go play around with one of my little flings like I didn't care, and the second he came back, I dropped everything. No conversations. No boundaries. No closure. Just access.

He hurt me, and I pretended nothing happened. Because expressing myself never felt safe. I couldn't look like I cared too much, and I didn't want to make waves. Somewhere deep down, I still believed if I just stayed quiet and stayed loyal—he'd finally choose me. But he never did. And honestly? I never chose me either.

Grasping for Straws

So right after that, I found my newest fling: a rapper, a thug, a man who paid me nooo mind. Lol. Someone to chase. And of course, I did just that. The situation didn't last long, but it showed how my dating behaviors were becoming riskier and riskier. This man had me riding around strapped and even took me on a mission to conduct interrogations.

One day, I went over, leaving work just to be with him whenever he asked or needed. Picking him up from long nights at the casino, doing whatever it took to be close to him. I don't even know why. Maybe it was the companionship. The sex wasn't good, but I just needed something in that moment—another empty connection filled with chasing and competing, only with even less compatibility. It was like I was just grasping for straws.

Then he went to jail—and you know what jail niggas do. He loved meeeee. I was sooo delusional, it's cringe. But at the time, it felt perfect. I got the emotional connection I thought I needed, without any of the reality attached. He was in jail, and so was my birthday twin, so I stayed on jail calls like it was normal life.

Collin: My Life Raft

Now, jail niggas were a thing; I cannot make this up. I had Collin—and yes, he saved me. Before him I was spiraling: drinking, drugging, partying, numb. I didn't even know who I was, performing life while secretly dying inside. But baby Collin woke me up; he became the mirror I couldn't ignore. His presence forced me to look at myself—all of me. Not the pretty version, not the party girl, not Shantrece; the broken girl trying to rebuild.

Once I became a mother, I started winning—slowly, quietly, consistently. My career was climbing, my voice getting louder; I was becoming exactly who I needed to be, for him and for me. Yet when it came to love, I was still at a loss. I craved care, intimacy, safety. I wanted someone to choose me—publicly, proudly, fully—but the men I entertained no longer did it for me; their games were tired, their stories recycled. For the first time, I noticed the shift: I wanted more.

Here's the part I didn't say out loud: I wasn't sure I deserved more. Underneath the progress I still carried shame—shame from the side-chick seasons, from the men I played, the hearts I hurt, the lies I told, the masks I wore. I feared real love and real connection; I believed that's when the karma would come, when I'd get what I gave, when someone would finally break me the way I'd broken others. So I stayed guarded—half in, half out—longing to be loved while keeping people at arm's length, sabotaging the very thing I swore I wanted.

And this is where the real work began: not just becoming a good mom, not just building a career, but unlearning the idea that I had to earn love; finally believing I was worthy of it, just as I am.

* * *

TRENCH LESSON

Lesson Learned:

Motherhood saved me, but it didn't erase the wounds. Collin gave me a mirror, but I still had to face myself. Healing begins when you stop chasing love in others and start anchoring yourself in your own worth.

Reflection Questions:

- What parts of yourself have you been abandoning just to feel chosen?
- How do you respond when love feels inconsistent—cling tighter, or shut down?
- What would choosing yourself look like in this season of your life?

Survival Strategy:

Shift the energy. Instead of chasing people who breadcrumb you, pour that same energy into building yourself. Anchor in routines, self-care, and relationships that actually nourish you. Don't confuse survival with peace—real love doesn't require you to shrink.

Affirmation:

"I am no longer chasing the possibility of love. I am worthy of love, safety, and peace as I am."

Your Reflection:

Alright, it's your turn. Use the space below to respond to the Trench Lesson activity and be real with yourself—no filters, no judgment.

_____

_____

_____

_____

_____

_____

_____

_____

_____

_____

_____

_____

_____

_____

_____

_____

_____

_____

_____

_____

_____

_____

_____

_____

_____

_____

_____

_____

_____

CHAPTER 9
SAFE HAVEN: THE ATTACK ON THE INNOCENT

Love came to rescue, but destructive behaviors were still present. I was still bleeding. Protective factors and survival behaviors were still active—even though safety had finally arrived. The same old coping skills that once kept me alive were now causing damage.

I belittled, manipulated, and took advantage of him. Shantrece was her strongest here—quick to clap back, quick to down-talk. Always prepared for war. She would tear him down just to glorify myself and my ability to "ho handle." She wasn't loving, she was defending.

But the truth? There was no enemy in front of me anymore. The battle wasn't with him. It was with me—my attachments, my fears, my own unhealed wounds. But in truth, this chapter revealed the truth about my attachments and the war within me. It was here I began to identify defense mechanisms that were still alive in me, to name my anxious attachment style, and to admit my self-injurious behaviors.

I found it—love finally came. But ummmm… is this really the love I was supposed to have? Because people with insecure attachment don't know how to just receive love. We question it. Overanalyze it. Minimize it. Pretend we don't even want it—right when it finally shows up.

We say we want love. We cry for it. Pray for it. Write about it in journals. Beg God for someone who sees us, holds us, chooses us. But when it comes? Whew. That's when the anxiety kicks in. That's when the "what ifs" get loud.

- *What if they leave?*
- *What if it's not real?*
- *What if they only love the version of me I showed them?*

So instead of leaning into love, we push it away. We start finding flaws in the other person. We get cold, distant, dismissive. We convince ourselves it's "too much" or "too soon." We tell ourselves we don't care—even when our hearts are screaming that we do. And if we don't sabotage it directly, we downplay it. We minimize the connection. We act unbothered. We tell our friends it's casual when we're low-key obsessed. We act like we're not invested to protect ourselves from the heartbreak we're already preparing for.

Because real love feels dangerous when you've spent your life learning that love always comes with pain, rejection, or abandonment.

It's not that we're unlovable. It's that we never learned how to feel safe being loved.

And when this love came? I did everything above. In hindsight, I hated how I showed up in that relationship—and it was me. I ruined it. As soon as it started, I started sabotaging.

When Real Love Showed Up

This man had been at it for a while. He was in my DMs for months, and I ignored him. But he was funny. Eventually, we started having conversations. He wasn't my type, and he was older. Then one day, my tire went flat. He said, "Let me come get your car. You take mine to work, and I'll get your tire fixed."

WHATTTT. A problem solver. He did for me what I had always done for other people. Baby, I was hooked.

This man swooped in and studied me. He attended to me and supported me. I was in my master's program and working two jobs while we were together, and I honestly believe it was because of him that I was able to do it. He made sure I had everything I needed. This was a MAN. He studied me. There wasn't a thing I wanted that he didn't get for me. *Destiny's Child's "Cater 2 U"* was the theme.

I gained so much weight—he kept me fed and happy. Then again, he was also a little crazy, and for me, that was a plus. I was happy. But you knooooow…

Once I started to really like him, my brain said, *but.*

- *But he's older.*
- *But he did over 15 years in jail.*
- *But he's ugly.*
- *But he's got the craziest baby mother drama.*

This lady left their kids on the doorstep. And what did I do? I raised them like they were mine. Did she appreciate it? Nope. She hacked his Facebook and leaked my nudes. That lady was nuts, but that added some "excitement."

Things were good. I had the family. But then here came Shantrece.

Choosing Chaos Over Peace

I started to compare him to other people. Compared him to Home Base. Told myself he wasn't as good because he wasn't my friend like Home Base was. But in hindsight? My old head ate that man up. He was a provider, making twice as much as Home Base—fresh out of prison. And he could've kicked Home Base's ass. But I put that other man up on a pedestal for nothing.

This is why I hate hindsight—because in the moment, despite getting the love I had always said I wanted—the kind that gave me everything I needed, calm, consistent, honest—I still didn't know how to handle it. No guessing, no games. And yet, part of me didn't know what to do with peace. Based on my attachment style and lived experiences, dysfunction felt like home.

So when peace showed up, it felt foreign. I questioned it. Called it boring. I didn't trust it. My nervous system was wired for survival, not safety, so even when I knew this love was good for me, I still craved the emotional highs and lows that had defined my past. I didn't feel worthy of love that didn't make me prove myself.

I kept waiting for it to fall apart. Kept pulling back just in case. That's what insecure attachment does—it makes you crave the familiar, even when it's dysfunctional.

The Fallout

So I began dismantling this relationship. It had already started on the heels of my jail relationship, and I was still entertaining others. I would talk badly about him to other people, making myself believe I didn't need him. That kept me "safe."

It didn't help that my oldest sister didn't want me with him. She warned me he was trouble and that it wouldn't end well. I took her words and added them to my own negative thoughts and behaviors, and I began withdrawing. This was my pattern: I would get with someone, love them so hard, cater to their every need—and then, boom. I'd pull away. I'd detach.

I didn't break them down to be mean, but I had to make them negative in my head in order to detach. And detach, I did. He even told me, "You're chasing those niggas, and they don't love you like I do. I'll let you go and see." And we did just that.

But then—boom.

Remember my sister said he was trouble? That trouble showed up. My door got kicked in. My phone was tapped. And my life changed forever. Me included. I lost everyone. I was all alone.

I had always had ADHD, but now anxiety showed up. Panic attacks too. I didn't feel safe. And you know where I went? Back.

The Attack on the Innocent

Before we go there, I have to acknowledge my faults. That man was not the target—this happened because I didn't love myself. I didn't feel worthy of his love. So I attacked him. He didn't deserve it. He was the innocent bystander caught in the crossfire of wounds he didn't create.

Love had finally come to rescue me, but I was still bleeding. My destructive behaviors didn't disappear just because I felt safe. I was still guarded. Still operating out of fear. Still wearing the armor of a warrior who didn't realize the war was over.

Shantrece was at her strongest here—quick with the clapback, always in control, always two steps ahead. I belittled him to glorify myself. Minimized his efforts to exaggerate my strength. Treated him like a threat instead of a partner, because I was still in survival mode. I made fun of him for loving me. Of course I did cause my core beliefs about myself was created from abandonment. I believed the stuck thought that I was unworthy of love or hard to love... so when love came around of course it wasn't real cause how could someone really love me when I was unworthy of love. His love contradicted my core beliefs.

One day, he went through my phone and found me talking to my coworker about him. Then, when the rapper came home, I went to see him—and got caught in two seconds. This man was monitoring the whole situation from my Apple Watch.

Caught. And still... he loved me.

He never deserved any of that. Because why would I leave a house where I was well taken care of to go chase chaos? But chaos was my comfort zone.

Facing Myself

Even in love, my protective patterns were alive and well. I had learned to use detachment, control, and criticism as shields. Those same defense mechanisms that once kept me alive were now destroying the very love I claimed to want.

This relationship forced me to face the truth about my attachment style—anxious, reactive, afraid of being too much and not enough all at once. And I saw how self-injurious my behaviors were—emotionally, mentally, spiritually.

I was fighting ghosts in a relationship that wasn't haunted.

But healing requires truth. And the truth is—I had finally found peace, and I didn't know how to live in it. Not yet. This chapter of my life showed me that love alone isn't enough. You have to believe you're worthy of it. You have to be ready to receive it without attacking it. Because even when love is real, if the wounds are still open, you'll bleed all over the person trying to hold you.

And that's exactly what I did.

The war wasn't over. I had just changed battlefields.

But this time, I started to see it.

I started to name it.

* * *

TRENCH LESSON

Lesson Learned:

Even when love is real, unhealed wounds can turn it into a battlefield. I learned that peace felt unsafe because my nervous system was wired for chaos. Instead of receiving love, I attacked it. The truth is, love alone isn't enough—you have to believe you're worthy of it, or you'll bleed on the people trying to hold you.

Reflection Questions:

- Do you find yourself doubting love even when it shows up consistently?
- In what ways do you push away the very things you've prayed for?
- What defense mechanisms are you still using that may be harming your current or future relationships?

Survival Strategy:

Start by naming your patterns. When you feel yourself withdrawing, criticizing, or sabotaging, pause and ask, *"Am I protecting myself—or pushing away safety?"* Replace old scripts with small acts of vulnerability. Let love in one step at a time—without demanding perfection, but with honesty and accountability. Healing is learning to trust peace even when chaos feels familiar.

Affirmation:

"I am worthy of safe, consistent, lasting love. I no longer attack the very things sent to heal me."

Your Reflection:

Alright, it's your turn. Use the space below to respond to the Trench Lesson activity and be real with yourself—no filters, no judgment.

_____

_____

_____

_____

_____

_____

_____

_____

_____

_____

_____

_____

_____

_____

_____

_____

_____

_____

_____

_____

_____

_____

_____

_____

_____

_____

_____

CHAPTER 10
RETURN TO HOME BASE

So the shit had finally hit the fan. Life had changed for me drastically. I didn't know whether I was coming or going. I had lost everything. I had moved into my own place—me and Collin starting over. I was finally a licensed therapist in the state of Maryland, no longer commuting to D.C. Money was being made. But given the last few months, I was a wreck.

My house had been raided. My cell phone records subpoenaed. My car had a tracker on it. And Mello was gone.

Mello had always been my protector. He was one of the reasons I was able to keep dudes at a distance—because I had him. We hung out, we spent time together, and he made me feel safe. Now, that was all gone.

Starting over was rough, but if you've been paying attention, you know I was never really alone. Because even when life forced me to retreat and regroup, I always found myself circling back to the same battlefield.

And this time, the war zone wasn't just in the streets, it was in my heart. Because when Home Base called, I answered. And just like that, I was back in the fight I swore I had left behind.

He wasn't in a relationship, and I was questioning mine. He said, "Come," and I came. I told my old head it wasn't working out and started creeping. The very first chance I got, I had Home Base meet me at a hotel while I was on a work trip. He came, and then it was off to the races. The moment I got with him, nothing else mattered.

If you were close to me, you knew—no one else had the same effect on me as this man. The moment he came around, I was a giddy 15-year-old girl again. In many ways, more than one. It was almost like we were stuck in time. Every time we got together, I felt like that wide-eyed teenager, desperate and waiting to be chosen.

It was like stepping into a time machine that erased all the growth, all the healing, all the logic. Around him, I didn't just feel young—I felt small. Because he was never just a man to me; he was the blueprint. The first one who made me feel seen, even if it was on his terms.

And no matter how much time passed, a part of me still needed his validation to feel whole.

But why? Because that version of me—the teenager who didn't know her worth—never got closure. She stayed frozen in time, hoping that one day he'd come back and finally love her the right way.

Every time he returned, it wasn't about the present—it was about trying to rewrite the past. I didn't want him. I wanted to heal the girl who needed him.

Nothing changed. No matter how long we were apart, we fell right back in.

I used to think it was because we both felt like we belonged to each other. I saw him as my everything. My brain had created a version of him that superseded reality. I built this "super person" in my head and got addicted to him because my body knew him—on a cellular level.

My brain had built deep neural pathways around him, formed from years of repetition, drama, and reconciliation. Every time we connected—no matter how toxic—it reinforced the pathway. Over time, my nervous system didn't just recognize him; it anticipated him. Being around him triggered familiarity, which my anxious attachment system translated as safety.

In *Attached*, Amir Levine explains how anxiously attached people tend to perform in relationships: we overfunction. We try harder, love louder, give more—just to maintain the bond. And when that bond feels threatened, we spiral. We obsess, analyze, overreach—all in an effort to soothe the panic.

I did all of that. I performed. I proved. I made myself necessary.

Even when he wasn't around, my mind kept him alive. That's what Levine calls the "phantom ex"—not because the person was perfect, but because they triggered our attachment system so intensely that we idolized them, even when the relationship was painful.

But the truth? I wasn't really in love with him. I was in love with the version of him I created in my mind—the man I needed him to be. I built a whole fantasy around him and called it love. And every time he came back, it was time for our show to begin.

Ughhh, hindsight. I wish I had known. I thought it was love.

So when the chance came, I ran. I left my old head and went straight "home."

It also didn't help that my life was falling apart, which sent me running right into his arms. I thought this was fate.

But my old head had warned me: *"They don't love you. If they did, they'd be with you. You're going to find out and you'll be back. You need to get that out of your system."*

Those were his exact words.

Y'all know I didn't listen.

There was never a storyline in my head where I thought we wouldn't be together. My thoughts were always, *We'll go explore the world, mess with other people, and when we're done, we'll circle back to each other.* And now? Now was the time he needed me.

He wasn't himself. You could tell his child's mother had hurt him. He was this smaller, less confident version of himself. He was working, but not making much. He was staying with friends, living in his car when they broke up. Things were bad—so bad he could barely feed himself. There were points where he literally lived out of his car.

How dare she put him out? He was the father of their children. I was outraged.

He was doing security and DoorDash just to get by. He told me there were times he had to DoorDash just to eat. He was down bad.

I didn't care. I didn't judge him. I just wanted to help.

By the time we started dealing with each other again, he had moved back in with his mom. His car had gone out, so he was using hers. She tried to control him. And you already know—*not my baby.* After all that he had gone through, I was pissed I couldn't be there for him. There I was, being catered to by someone else, while the man I loved was going through hell. *How dare me.*

He didn't have anything, but I loved him more than the man who gave me the world.

So I figured out how to help him. She wasn't about to play with mine. I let him use my car. I let him stay over whenever he wanted to get away. I was cooking, cleaning, and playing Susie Homemaker.

Things were going good. This was the life I wanted.

Losing My Mother

And then, here came another whirlwind. I lost my mother.

That loss cracked something open in me that I didn't even know I was still holding on to. She was the first person I ever chased love from, the first person I ever needed to prove myself to—and now, she was gone.

When she passed, we weren't even speaking. I kept wondering if she knew that I loved her. My anger had robbed me of the chance to have one last conversation with my mom.

I remember being in the house for days—numb, not eating, not even combing my hair.

And right on cue, Home Base was there.

You couldn't tell me God didn't send him to help me through it. He was there, combing my hair, sitting with me in silence. At the time, that small act felt like love. But when I look back with clarity, I see the truth: he wasn't at the funeral. He didn't show up for the repast. He didn't even bring me flowers.

The emotional weight of that loss was mine to carry alone. But somehow, just his presence—bare minimum and all—was enough for me then.

Because I was vulnerable. Because I was grieving the first person who made me feel like I had to earn love... while holding onto the man who kept making me prove it.

We made it through that season, and it only became clearer to me that I needed him.

Falling Into Old Roles

Then one day, I was minding my business on God's internet when this young girl from around the way added me to her Close Friends. It was strange because I knew her, but we weren't cool. And then I saw it— she posted a pic of him and her.

You know me—I hit him up, told him to get that shit under control. Of course, he told me it was nothing. They were just cool. And I believed him, because she was young and funny-looking. There was no way he was really entertaining her.

Then his ex started flirting with him on Facebook. A lot of little things were happening, but I still didn't see. In my head, I had my man, my man, my man. But with all of that going on, I still needed reassurance. I had grown enough to know not to take no shit. It was like, "Okay, we've been talking too long—either shit or get off the pot." So, he goes on vacation, and I tell him straight up: "I need something more. We're grown now. If you're not ready, let's stop talking." And he says, *"I'll give you more."*

Boom—we're together, y'all.

But the truth? When we got back together as adults, I slipped right back into my old role: planner, fixer, backbone. I started mapping out his life before he even asked. "Get your full CDL, babe—bigger checks, better hours. But first, we'll get you a car." On the surface, it sounded supportive. But underneath, it was classic codependency.

In a codependent pair, there's an over-functioner (me) and an under-functioner (him). The over-functioner feels valuable by steering, saving, financing, motivating. The under-functioner stays comfortable letting someone else handle the heavy lifts.

My anxious attachment system equated usefulness with worth. So the more I invested, the safer I felt. His under-functioning fed that cycle, because every time he leaned on me, my role was confirmed.

The dynamic looked healthy—"I just want the best for him"—but it quietly eroded boundaries. I used his progress as proof I was indispensable. The thing was, he lacked desire and motivation. Then, you know I had to explore. He failed his first CDL test and didn't think he was capable.

Looking back, he had never really gotten anything for himself. His mother was vital in creating his life. Then his child's mother. He always lived in the shadow of others—always somebody's "homeboy." And here I was, loving a man with no plan. I loved men with plans. But even without one, I was still invested. I thought, "If I just give him the plan, we'll be good."

But I was messing things up before they even started. My anxious attachment style and codependency were in full drive. When a woman helps a man too much—especially in a way that takes over responsibility for his progress—it can backfire emotionally and psychologically. I was too far in my masculine energy.

While the intent might be love, support, or partnership, for many men—especially those still developing their identity or struggling with self-worth—it doesn't feel like love. It feels like pressure. Or worse, emasculation. And he was definitely struggling. Now that I think of it, he never knew who he was. I watched him become like whoever his best friend was at the time.

And I was repeating what his mom had always done—managing, controlling, shaping. Every time I took the wheel—managing his goals, handling his business, fronting money—he was receiving a silent message: "You can't do this on your own." Even if I never said it directly, my actions screamed it.

Over time, that creates resentment or quiet withdrawal. A man might start avoiding conversations about progress, money, or growth —not because he doesn't care, but because it triggers feelings of failure. And in relationships where masculinity is tied to providing or leading, too much help feels like subtle disrespect. It also disrupts the balance of desire. Men often feel most drawn to women when they feel purposeful and confident. But when a woman becomes too responsible for his life, it kills polarity. He doesn't feel like the man—and eventually, she doesn't feel like the woman.

So while "helping" might feel like love to her, to him, it feels like being managed, corrected, even castrated. This was a recipe for disaster. Because helping? That's the way I love.

The Unraveling

Things started quietly unraveling. I noticed him pulling away, and soon uncovered a major miscommunication. He was getting distant. Then we were talking and, y'alllll, I played myself HARD. Remember when I asked for more and he said he would give it to me? Yup. Turns out he meant he would give me "more," but not the relationship. I thought he meant he wanted to be with me. Nope, not the case.

But you know me—I said, *That's fine. Let's not do that. I don't want you to feel pressured. We can take a step back.* Look at me compromising. My dumb ass should have left at that point. Nooo. Instead, I made a post about our relationship, and the bitch didn't even like it. That should've told me everything I needed to know. But y'all know… hindsight.

Grey Rock Survival

One thing about my God—He protects me. He moves mountains to protect me. We were going through the motions, but I was a little more adult now. I started taking space. He stopped calling, I didn't call. We only talked if he engaged. I was being a grey rock.

The "grey rock" method is a self-protection strategy used in relationships—especially with toxic, manipulative, or narcissistic individuals—where you intentionally become emotionally dull and unresponsive to avoid feeding drama or conflict. The goal is to become so boring and neutral that the other person loses interest in provoking or manipulating you. Instead of arguing or defending yourself, you give short, factual answers.

It works because people who thrive on control or emotional chaos often feed off your reactions. If you stop reacting, they eventually stop pushing. But let's be clear—grey rocking is a survival tool, not a healthy long-term communication style. And in my case, it didn't help, because my feelings were never truly communicated.

I remember one time I tried to talk, and this man said, *"Let's do it first."* Bruhhh. The ghetto. But like I said, my God wasn't going to let me have this man—no matter how hard I tried. God's next move dismantled the entire program. The veil was lifted. It hurt like hell, but it had to happen.

His mother died a year after mine. Whatttt—you couldn't tell me God didn't bring us together to help us heal together. I jumped right in, started planning, helping, showing up. But this man started pushing me out. Stopped answering me. Had a whole breakdown and his friends called me.

I went over—and he still ignored me. I'm talking about me, on the porch, trying to get through. I wrote him this long letter about being there for him. The whole ordeal was embarrassing. I fought for a spot in his process. And what did I get? A half ass letter about being there for him. No introduction to his family. It was clear.

I was still there, but I definitely fell back.

Cracks in the Fantasy

We were back to our on-and-off thing, but now it was really off. Then one day, he reached out—I think it was around Valentine's Day. Mind you, we hadn't been talking. But he needed to do something with his mother's estate and needed a ride. Of course, I took him.

I went over, he cooked for me, and then I went home. I thought, "Okay, we're moving different now."

This was the first time I had seen him in a while. He had finished his mother's house with her insurance money. I wondered what he would do with it. Honestly, I always felt like when he got money, he'd look out for me since I always looked out for him.

When he first got that money, he bought me two things from Milano. And that was it—compared to all I had done for him. I redid that man's entire wardrobe. I hated how he dressed, so I was always buying him what I wanted him to have. I got him his first pair of Timberlands, his first pair of Yeezys. And he didn't even think to look out for me.

It's crazy—I can look on his page today and still see him rocking the fits I put together.

The truth? He was never going to be the person I needed him to be. I used to think he didn't do it for me because he didn't have it. Nope. He just didn't care. And there was no way my God was going to let me end up with him.

But I still wasn't listening. I entertained him whenever he said hello. I stopped reaching out, but when he reached out, I always thought it meant he was ready now.

Lol. Nope. He was just checking to see if I was still stupid.

And, baybeeee, one day—I was not.

I confronted him. Outed him. And then I got word he was still on Snapchat posting pics with the same girl he swore he didn't deal with. So I hit him like, "Stop playing in my face. If you want that, leave me the fuck alone."

The Shattering

BABYYYY, that man masked up and came for blood. He thought he ate.

He said, "I would have to be in ya face to play in ya face. I don't deal with you. I hit you every now and again. I was just dealing with you in between ya jail niggas."

And that was the last thing he said to me. Easter 2023.

That moment broke something in me. I dropped the phone and immediately cried—loud, ugly, guttural sobs. The only man I had ever truly loved, the one I built my entire blueprint for love around, had just told me it was never real. That love I had been chasing, sacrificing for, defending, and idolizing—it was fiction. A story I told myself to survive. And with one sentence, he shattered it. The illusion, the hope, the little girl inside me who waited for him to finally choose her… gone.

I spiraled. Every dark, hidden belief I carried about myself rushed to the surface: *You're unlovable. You're always too much or not enough. You'll never be chosen. You were a placeholder, not a partner.* It wasn't just a breakup —it was confirmation. It was evidence that my worst fears were true. The pain wasn't just about him; it was about everything. Every moment I ignored red flags. Every time I overperformed. Every time I stayed silent just to keep the peace. It felt like I was mourning not just the relationship but also the years I lost trying to earn a love that never truly existed.

This is the core of Relationship Traumatic Stress Syndrome (RTSS) —the chronic emotional injury caused by long-term exposure to unhealthy love. It's not just heartbreak; it's psychological trauma. RTSS teaches you to question your reality. It blurs the line between manipulation and passion, inconsistency and intimacy, neglect and normalcy. I didn't just lose a man—I lost the foundation I had built my self-worth on.

RTSS leaves behind debris: hypervigilance, fear of vulnerability, people-pleasing, emotional numbing, avoidance, shame. And this breakup? It activated every single symptom. Suddenly it felt confirmed that love wasn't safe. It wasn't desirable. It was dangerous. It was a setup. The next man who tried to love me never even had a chance, because I had already decided that love wasn't real. The version I thought was real turned out to be a lie.

But in the middle of that pain, something else happened too. The veil lifted. I saw him—not as the man I loved, but as the mirror I used to avoid looking at myself. The truth? I created the fantasy. I gave him credit for a version of love he never offered. I stayed loyal to a story that was never mutual. And when the truth dropped, it hurt like hell— but it also gave me clarity. I was free. Not from him, but from the delusion.

The Beginning of Me

The ending of that relationship didn't just confirm my fears—it forced me to confront them. It revealed the parts of me that still believed I needed to be broken to be lovable, that I had to earn love through suffering. But it also gave me a starting point. A place to begin again. To define love for myself—not through pain, but through truth, safety, and choice.

That was the death of the illusion. And the beginning of me.

One of the wildest things about toxic relationships—especially ones wrapped in trauma bonds—is how you can be fully aware and completely blind at the same time. That was me. I knew something wasn't right. My gut would whisper it. My discernment would show up like clockwork—flagging red flags, catching inconsistencies, reading the energy shifts. But somehow, I'd still talk myself out of it. I'd override that inner knowing with doubt, excuses, and his words.

That was the real betrayal—not what he did to me, but what I kept doing to myself. Picking him over my own intuition. Over my sanity. Over my peace.

I think back to the time one of his own friends tried to put me on game. Told me flat out, "He treats her like a dummy. He doesn't even care for her like that." And when I told Home Base, expecting some type of outrage, some type of "how dare he talk about you like that"—I got the opposite. Nothing. A shrug. A lie that it wasn't true. No fire. No protection. No defense.

But still, I believed him. Why? Because I wanted to. Because the version of him that loved me was more comforting than the truth of him that didn't. I convinced myself that his friend must be lying, jealous, messy—anyone but him. I chose the lie because it made staying easier.

That's what toxic love does—it confuses the hell out of you. The highs create so much emotional intensity that you mistake it for depth. And when it's good, it's good enough to cloud the bad. He was never cruel in obvious ways. He wasn't violent. He didn't curse me out. When people would say he was mean, I never saw it.

He hurt me with passivity. With silence. With just enough affection to keep me questioning myself instead of him. The absence of overt mistreatment became the thing I used to convince myself it wasn't abuse.

I ask myself all the time—how did I stay so long? But when I look closer, I remember: he always had the story. Always had a way to make me doubt my own memory, my own feelings. He was gentle with his manipulation, and that's the kind that hits the hardest.

The delusion didn't come from nowhere—it was maintained, fed, and performed so well it became believable. Until it wasn't. After his mom died, I think he just didn't have the energy to keep up the act. The charm started to dull. And once the illusion wore off, so did the love.

That's what made it all so disorienting—because I didn't fall in love with who he really was. I fell in love with who he presented himself to be. With the idea. The potential. The performance. And when it ended, I wasn't just grieving him—I was grieving the part of me that wanted to believe him. The part that kept choosing the story over myself.

SN: Vulnerability is a beast. It exposes the parts of you that you usually keep tucked away—the fear, the shame, the deep ache for connection. Writing this chapter forced me to look those parts square in the face and to be real with myself in a way I usually avoid. This wasn't easy. In fact, this was the hardest chapter to write. Not because of him, but because of me. Because I had to peel back the armor and finally tell the truth—not the cute, well-packaged version I use to protect my pride, but the messy, raw, unfiltered version that bleeds.

Let me make something very clear: this chapter ain't about no one man. No one person holds that kind of power over my life. This isn't about Home Base, or the heartbreak he caused, or even the lies he told. This was never about him. He was just the mirror. The spark. The vessel. The catalyst God used to show me everything I still hadn't healed. Everything I still believed about myself that was rooted in abandonment, rejection, and fear.

He didn't break me—I was already cracked. He just found the fault lines.

And to whoever's reading this thinking it's about you—you were just a part of the pattern. A symptom, not the source. The real work? That was always between me and my wounds. Because healing ain't about blaming—it's about understanding. And I had to understand why I kept choosing people who reflected my pain back to me. Why I kept showing up to relationships already bleeding, already doubting, already feeling not enough.

I didn't write this to drag anyone. I wrote it to free myself. To speak the truth out loud, so it doesn't keep whispering in the dark. Vulnerability, for me, isn't about weakness—it's about finally owning my story.

And this chapter? It's not about a man. It's about the moment I realized I'd been carrying the weight of my past in every relationship I'd ever had. And now… I'm ready to put it down

* * *

TRENCH LESSON

Lesson Learned:

Toxic love isn't about the other person—it's about the wounds they mirror back to you. The real betrayal is when you abandon your own intuition just to hold onto the story you want to believe. Healing begins when you choose to see the truth, even when it hurts.

Reflection Questions:

- Have you ever ignored your intuition because believing the lie felt easier?
- What stories have you been telling yourself about love that might be illusions?
- How can you start honoring your discernment instead of silencing it?

Survival Strategy:

Start practicing radical honesty—with yourself first. Journal the red flags you see and the excuses you make for them. When the narrative in your head doesn't match the reality in front of you, choose reality. That's where freedom begins.

Affirmation:

"I no longer cling to illusions. I honor my truth, trust my spirit, and release the love that requires me to abandon myself."

Your Reflection:

Alright, it's your turn. Use the space below to respond to the Trench Lesson activity and be real with yourself—no filters, no judgment.

_____

_____

_____

_____

_____

_____

_____

_____

_____

_____

_____

_____

_____

_____

_____

_____

_____

_____

_____

_____

_____

_____

_____

_____

_____

_____

_____

_____

_____

_____

_____

CHAPTER 11
I CAN FINALLY HEAL

My brain couldn't rest—it was working overtime. I was in a full-blown spiral, the kind that steals your appetite and your sleep. This felt like being ambushed on the battlefield. This… this right here was the reason I avoided love. Because when I love, I love hard. Deep. Reckless. I thought I did my big one by guarding my heart, and honestly, I did a damn good job. Nobody had ever made me crash out before.

But this man? He took me there. And the part that pissed me off the most was that I didn't see it coming. What he did to me is what I had done to people. How the hell did he pull a me on me?

That was the betrayal that cut the deepest—me betraying myself. Because somewhere deep down, I did see it coming. I never fully cut off Honey, and I ran into my birthday twin during the chaos. My intuition wasn't broken—it was whispering. But I didn't want to hear it. I was in too deep.

On the surface, I was heartbroken. I couldn't make sense of the intensity of the pain. But the truth? It was my ego. It was the perception. The embarrassment. How was it that everyone seemed to know how he really felt except me? I felt like a fool.

What made it worse was that my love was real. I was real. I wanted to be there for him. I believed in him. And he used me. He used me for my energy—just like one of his exes said he did to her. She told me once that he drained her, and I finally understood what she meant. I hated that I thought I was different. That because we were friends, I was safe.

But I wasn't.

He talked about his kids' mothers to me, calling them freaks. Why wouldn't he talk about me the same way? He even told me once that he used to hit one of them in the car because she was "a hoe." *This* was the man I trusted with my heart. The regret ate me alive. I should've seen it. I knew better. But my trust in him clouded everything—my intuition, my discernment— gone.

When he said those words to me, the veil was lifted. I was no longer stupid—let me stop. Love can definitely make us feel stupid, but what I've learned is that love gives us tunnel vision—both scientifically and emotionally.

When we're in love, our brains flood with feel-good chemicals like dopamine and oxytocin. These light up the reward centers and make us crave more of that connection. Meanwhile, the prefrontal cortex— the part of the brain responsible for judgment and critical thinking— literally shuts down. That means red flags start to look pink, gut instincts get ignored, and flaws become romanticized. We only see what we want to see.

Love creates a chemical high that blinds us to reality, pushing us to idolize our partner and overlook anything that threatens the fantasy. It's not just emotional—it's neurological. That's why we stay too long, forgive too much, and believe in people who have already shown us who they are.

Now, add that to my delusion and attachment issues and boom— disaster.

But here's the part that gave me peace: I realized it wasn't just him —it was my brain. That insight alone was healing.

I had started to obsess, thinking that because I couldn't stop thinking about him, it meant he was "the one." But what I was feeling wasn't destiny—it was my dysregulated nervous system. Those butterflies? That was my body's fight-or-flight system firing off. And once I understood that, I could finally breathe. But I was still in pain.

Running to the Altar

I found myself at the altar, and baby, I ran.

This wasn't a walk. This wasn't a gentle stroll to the front of a church pew. I ran to that altar like my life depended on it—because it did. I was in so much pain I could barely breathe. The kind of pain that steals your appetite, clouds your mind, and makes silence feel like punishment.

I hadn't felt hurt like that since my mother's funeral. My world shattered. The only man I believed loved me never did. The love I had been holding on to for nearly two decades was never even mine. And the place I used to run to when everything fell apart? Home Base? He was gone.

There was no Mello. No best friend to call. No one to run to. Except God.

And when I say I met God at that altar, I mean it. I sobbed. I released. I laid my pain down and said, *"God, I can't do this anymore. Take it."* And He did.

It didn't erase the pain instantly, but it shifted something inside me. For once, I stopped fighting for people and started fighting for *myself*.

My honey came back around, as he always seemed to, right on time. He filled that space temporarily, giving me that comfort I craved. But something had changed. I had changed. I couldn't even be with him. I knew he always wanted and craved love, but I had to be honest. I could never trust him to love me again. I just craved his attention at times. Knowing I really had no intentions of loving him, I created distance.

Because I was doing something better.

I got a better job. I started reading again. I created content again. I was remembering who I was before the heartbreaks, before the betrayals. I wasn't just surviving anymore—I was rebuilding.

Healing as a Daily Practice

Mental health became my lifeline. I started digging into the work. I read Amir Levine's *Attached* and cried when I saw myself on every page. I finally understood what it meant to have an anxious attachment style—that I wasn't "crazy" or "too much." I was just scared.

I had learned early that love wasn't consistent, so I chased it. I performed for it. I clung to emotionally unavailable men because they felt familiar. They mirrored the chaos I knew in childhood. But that chaos wasn't love—it was survival.

I learned to slow down, sit in my feelings, and trace them back to the source. I began to see my triggers clearly—rejection, abandonment, silence. And I stopped reacting and started reflecting.

Healing became a daily practice. Gym. Church. Work. Repeat. I moved my body and moved my spirit. I was shedding the layers that no longer served me. Every mile on the treadmill, every scripture I read, every journal entry—it was all working together to bring me back to me.

I saw Home Base for who he really was: a broken man who had never achieved anything of his own, who wore manipulation like cologne, who sold dreams he had no intention of delivering. And I thank God He didn't let me end up with him.

I would've spent my life pouring into a man with holes I didn't make—and I would've drowned trying to save him. As the smoke cleared, I realized he could never meet my needs because he never learned how to love beyond survival. He could never give me the kind of love I give—because he never learned how to receive it.

That man could not show up for me emotionally, mentally, or even materially. One of the ways I know I'm healing is that I now understand my love languages. Acts of service and gifts—they matter to me. They're how I feel seen and considered. And he never brought me flowers. Never celebrated me in the way I deserved. That wasn't oversight—that was his limit.

Had God given him to me, I would've been miserable.

So yes, I was hurt. Yes, I was embarrassed. But I was also free. For the first time, I wasn't in love with a fantasy. I was in love with my own healing.

So now what? I'm healed? Nah. But I'm healing—actively, intentionally, and unapologetically. And that is something.

I'm not the same girl who begged to be chosen. I'm not the woman who hid behind performance and people-pleasing. I've outgrown that version of myself. The woman I'm becoming? She's grounded. She's clear. She's at peace with who she is and what she's survived. She doesn't chase love—she attracts alignment. She's not desperate for attention—she's rooted in purpose.

And now I know what I want from a man—not just chemistry, not just attraction, but consistency. Emotional safety. Someone who knows how to communicate without punishing. A man who is self-aware, who knows how to love me without trying to save me or dim me down. I want mutual effort, mutual growth. Not someone to complete me—but someone to build with.

But let me be real—I'm not perfect. I've had to confront the ways I get in my own way. I can be guarded. I shut down when I feel misunderstood. I overthink everything. I still wrestle with codependency and the old urge to make someone else's feelings more important than my own. I can be emotionally impulsive and quick to assume.

That's my work. That's my growth edge.

Healing has taught me accountability. I now understand that no man will ever be enough if I still believe I'm not enough. I had to let go of the fantasy that someone else was going to fix me or make me feel whole. That was never their job—it's mine.

And that's what I've been doing. Reparenting myself. Sitting with my trauma, not running from it. Learning to be with my emotions without letting them control me. Because if I want a healthy relationship, I have to be a healthy version of myself.

Codependency taught me to confuse love with sacrifice. Trauma taught me to expect abandonment and prepare for pain. But healing? Healing is teaching me to choose myself first—without guilt. To trust myself. To believe that I deserve the kind of love that doesn't hurt. That doesn't require me to shrink or perform or bleed to prove my worth.

Becoming Her

So who am I now? I'm her. I'm the woman I prayed to become. Still soft. Still flawed. But self-aware. Self-loving. And on my way to receiving the kind of love I've been building within myself.

I am a woman who has had repeated traumatic experiences with love. Some of these experiences were from my own hand. My negative relationship dynamics and defense mechanisms created this dynamic. I learned to confuse chaos with connection, attention with affection, and performance with worth. I abandoned myself for the sake of being chosen. That wasn't just by accident—it was a survival strategy.

I became the girl who over-functioned, over-gave, and under-asked. I mirrored what I thought people wanted so they wouldn't leave. But in doing so, I kept leaving myself.

If you're wondering what Relationship Traumatic Stress Syndrome (RTSS) looks like in real time, this was it. These cycles—of craving love, chasing it, minimizing myself, attaching to dysfunction, confusing intensity with intimacy—this was RTSS in motion.

It wasn't just bad luck in love. It was a patterned response to emotional trauma that trained me to confuse pain with passion and inconsistency with connection.

I kept reenacting the same story with different characters, hoping for a new ending. But healing doesn't come from someone choosing you—it comes from you choosing yourself.

So if this sounds like your story too? Don't run from the pain. Sit with it. Study it. Heal it. You don't have to keep surviving love. You deserve to feel safe in it. And that starts with you.

* * *

TRENCH LESSON

Lesson Learned:

If you need someone to love you in order to feel okay, you'll always be vulnerable to the devastation of their absence. That kind of love isn't grounding—it's fragile, because it places your emotional stability in someone else's hands. When your self-worth is built on another person's validation, it isn't truly self-worth at all; it's dependency wrapped in the illusion of connection.

You are not needy, you are simply responding to a lifetime of unmet emotional needs, and your longing is a signal, not a flaw. Healing begins when you shift the focus from being chosen to choosing yourself first. When you stop waiting to be enough in someone else's eyes and start seeing yourself clearly through your own. Because secure attachment doesn't mean being perfect, never triggered, or always calm. It means creating safety within yourself first, so that love from others becomes an addition—not a lifeline.

Reflection Questions:

- Where have I confused chaos with love in my own story?
- What daily practices (journaling, prayer, movement) can help me ground myself in healing?
- What illusions about love am I still holding onto that I need to release?

Survival Strategy:

Stop outsourcing your wholeness. Anchor yourself in practices that regulate your nervous system and remind you that you're already enough. Therapy, prayer, journaling, rest, and self-compassion are your weapons. Healing is messy, but it's yours.

What does your new life look like. Who are you what do you do daily? Who are you around? Develop this new life so vividly.

Affirmation:

"I am healing. I am whole. I choose myself first, and in doing so, I create space for the love I truly deserve."

Your Reflection:

Alright, it's your turn. Use the space below to respond to the Trench Lesson activity and be real with yourself—no filters, no judgment.

_____

_____

_____

_____

_____

_____

_____

_____

_____

_____

_____

_____

_____

_____

_____

_____

_____

_____

_____

_____

_____

_____

_____

_____

_____

_____

_____

_____

_____

CHAPTER 12
THE ONE

The tears had finally stopped, and yes—I did feel better. But the stillness was dangerous. Stillness is when soldiers count the cost, when you look around the battlefield and ask yourself: how did I get so confused? I'm a therapist. I teach people about boundaries, red flags, attachment styles—and still, I let a pissy boy manipulate me. That realization sent me smooth off.

But here's the good part: I came out of this battle with questions instead of just scars. Usually after heartbreak, you go numb. Immobilized. You swear off love like it's the problem. But not me. I wasn't dead inside. Scared? Absolutely. But not shut down. There was still a flicker of hope, a willingness to learn.

Love, despite everything, still felt worth it. Too beautiful to give up on entirely.

I realized I had just never been taught how to choose love properly. I was choosing based on what felt familiar, not what felt safe. And that familiarity? That chaos? That wasn't chemistry—it was trauma dressed up like passion. So now I ask better questions:

- Does this person create safety or anxiety in me?
- Do I feel seen, or just used to being invisible?

- Do I actually like them, or am I chasing validation?

Clarity comes when you stop chasing the story and start sitting with the truth. That's where I am now—not bitter, just better. Not closed off, just careful. Still scared sometimes, but still open. Because this time? I'm not choosing from survival. I'm choosing from wholeness.

The first thing I had to do was clarify my misunderstandings. If what I thought was love wasn't, then I needed facts. And whenever I'm confused, I grab a book. During this stage, Gottman saved me.

Dr. John Gottman, one of the leading researchers in relationship psychology, teaches that true, lasting love is something we build through intentional acts—not just something we feel in fleeting moments. I used to think that if I felt love intensely and immediately, it meant something divine was happening—love at first sight, soul ties, twin flame energy. I thought that feeling was the universe confirming, *"This is the one."* But what I've learned the hard way is that fairy tales aren't real, and sometimes that intensity isn't love—it's familiarity.

And if someone feels familiar, you need to ask yourself: *Why?* Is it because they feel like home? Or is it because they feel like chaos disguised as comfort? Often, we confuse emotional intensity with compatibility, when in reality, our nervous system is just responding to something it's known before—dysregulation, inconsistency, emotional unavailability. That "spark" might be your trauma recognizing something it's already experienced, not some magical sign.

Familiarity can be a red flag, especially for those of us with trauma histories. Because what feels normal isn't always healthy—it's just what we've survived before.

At the heart of every healthy romantic relationship is a deep friendship. This friendship forms the foundation, built by truly knowing your partner's inner world—their hopes, fears, dreams, and day-to-day thoughts. Gottman calls this *building love maps,* and it's essential to maintaining emotional closeness.

Love also requires showing up for your partner in the small, everyday moments. It's not about grand gestures but about turning toward your partner—answering their bids for connection, offering a hug, sending a thoughtful message, or just listening. These consistent acts build what Gottman calls an *emotional bank account*—a reserve of goodwill that helps couples weather hard times.

And when conflict inevitably arises (because it always does), the key to lasting love isn't avoiding it—it's learning to repair. Healthy couples use repair attempts like humor, empathy, and compromise to find their way back to each other.

Gottman also emphasizes that love must feel emotionally safe. Criticism, contempt, defensiveness, and stonewalling—his "Four Horsemen of the Apocalypse"—erode that safety and predict the end of love if left unchecked. Replacing them with appreciation, accountability, and gentle communication is how love survives.

Above all, love is rooted in trust and commitment—believing your partner has your back, and choosing them every day, especially during the hard seasons. According to Gottman, love isn't perfect, but when two people are emotionally responsive, committed, and willing to grow together, it can absolutely last.

So once I had a working definition of what I was looking for, another question slowly crept in. *Was I worthy?*

Abso-fuckin-lutely.

I knew I was worthy now. But I was still doing mess. Doing the same shit the unhealed version of me would've done. I caught another body—yup, just because I heard it was good. And it was. But that's all it was—no consistency, no commitment. I was still saying I wanted one thing while doing another.

So what was the issue? I started to consider the relationship I had with myself. That question changed everything. I had spent so much time chasing love outside of me that I never stopped to nurture the one relationship that would carry me through every season: the one with me.

I had to learn what it meant to choose myself—not just in theory, but in daily, intentional moments that required me to pause and prioritize my own needs. I realized that self-love wasn't about being selfish or shutting others out—it was about finally letting *me* matter.

That's all that little girl inside me ever wanted. That's why she kept showing up, stealing the show, and doing whatever she needed to get what she thought she wanted. She needed me to speak for her, to fight for her, to give her what she needed. But I never did. And that's why I stayed broken.

So I began to ask myself the same questions I used to ask about men:

- Do I feel safe with me?
- Do I keep my promises to myself?
- Do I show up for myself emotionally, mentally, spiritually?

And the honest answer? Not always. I had abandoned myself so many times in the name of being chosen, being loved, or simply being enough. But now, I was learning to stay. I was learning to build trust within.

I started spending time alone not because I had to, but because I wanted to. I treated myself the way I had always longed for someone else to treat me—with gentleness, respect, consistency, and care.

It's Time to Love Me

Dating myself looked like buying flowers just to brighten my space. It meant solo dinners where I dressed up for me, no audience necessary. It meant putting my phone down and sitting with my thoughts—no numbing, no distractions. It meant setting boundaries and actually holding them. It meant not waiting for a man to take me on a trip or tell me I'm beautiful. I affirmed myself. I took myself out. I showed myself a good time. Most importantly, I kept my word to me.

But it went deeper than that. Self-care became soul care. I prayed. I journaled. I reflected. I forgave myself—for staying too long, for not knowing better, for abandoning the girl who just wanted to be loved. I realized I had to re-parent myself in the ways I wasn't nurtured. I had to become the woman my younger self needed—the mother, the friend, the protector. I poured into myself from a place of love, not punishment. Not fixing, but healing.

And slowly, my self-worth became internal, not circumstantial. It wasn't about who called, who stayed, or who saw me. It was about how deeply I had finally seen myself. That's what dating yourself really is. It's not a trend—it's a return. A return to self. A return to wholeness. A reclamation of all the love you so freely gave away without asking for any in return.

And now? I give that love to me first. Not last. Not in pieces. First. Because I deserve it. Because I am worth it. And because no matter who comes or goes, I'm not leaving me again. That was the vibe I was in. The energy I was in. And I was winning.

It Happened Again

I can't believe it. The hairs on the back of my neck stood up. *WTF? I know that ain't love's funky ass again.*

And it was.

Nooooo, I wasn't ready. I had just started loving me. I was in a good space and on a good path. The thought of love after everything I'd been through? Terrifying. When love shows up again after you've experienced relationship trauma, your brain doesn't always respond with excitement—it responds with warning signs.

Your body feels it first: that tightness in your chest, the urge to pull back, the way your heart races not just from butterflies but from fear. Your nervous system starts scanning for threats. Because the last time you let someone in, they didn't stay. Or worse—they stayed and broke you.

Your brain, trying to protect you, lights up the old neural pathways wired through past pain. The ones that say: *Don't trust this. Don't get too close. They'll leave. They'll lie.* It's not being dramatic—it's conditioning. Traumatic relationships create a loop where love gets tangled with abandonment, manipulation, and rejection. So now, when something or someone healthy shows up, your brain doesn't recognize it as safe. It registers it as unfamiliar, and unfamiliar feels dangerous.

You want love, but your brain has learned to equate closeness with chaos. And so—you guessed it—it was time to run. Not because I thought it wouldn't work, but because it *might* work. And if it did, it might cost me my peace. I didn't want to lose myself again or risk being left. Lord knows I wasn't ready for the merry-go-round.

But what can you do when love comes knocking?

I knew the old me would've trashed the person sent to love me simply because I wasn't ready. That version of me should've been long gone—but I didn't know how the new me would handle it. And that was even scarier.

You know how you can feel a shift before anyone says a word? That's what happened. The air got heavy, thick—like we both knew someone had crossed a line, even if nothing physical had happened yet. And I wasn't naïve anymore. Not after everything I'd been through. I knew exactly what that look meant.

Up until then, I had clung to the comfort of our friendship. It was safe. Familiar. Built on years of history and mutual care. He knew my scars. I knew his. So when the world felt unstable—after Mello dipped, after Home Base did what he always does—it made sense that I'd reach for something that felt steady. And honestly? It felt good to be cared for again.

But this time, there was something unspoken growing between us. And maybe I didn't want to admit it—because it complicated things. Because it meant re-evaluating what this relationship was and had always been.

Here's the truth: I've spent so long confusing familiarity with safety, loyalty with love, comfort with chemistry. I've been trying to rewrite my story while still holding on to all the old characters. And in that moment, watching his face change, I realized the plot was shifting again.

This wasn't just about him catching feelings. It was about me realizing that my boundaries had blurred. That maybe I liked the attention. Maybe I needed to feel chosen—even in the quietest way. Maybe I wasn't as healed as I thought.

Because this wasn't just "my dog" anymore. This was a man seeing me—not as a sister, not as a homie—but as a woman. And whether or not I was ready to see him the same way, I knew nothing would ever be the same after that look.

I was right— shit was different, and it was confirmed the night he stayed over. That wasn't strange in itself, but the way he held me was. You know he tried it. Umm, nope—not that easy. But the shift was undeniable. So we had the conversation, the one we couldn't avoid anymore. The elephant in the room had grown too big.

It was complicated. He had been telling his ex we weren't fucking around, and now here we were, admitting feelings for each other. We laid out the pros and cons, then said, *fuck it—we both deserve a fresh start.*

But my *fuck it* came with a heavy cross to bear. Being with him meant adding another layer of complication to my already tangled love history. Another person who knew somebody. Another homie. For years, people had whispered about me because I hung with all boys, but I had always taken pride in the fact that, out of all the men I called brother, I wasn't intimate with any of them… until now. What would people think if they found out?

And then there was the age gap—he was younger. The judgments. The rumors. The shame. My mind spun with all the reasons why this couldn't work. I told myself it was just my attachment system pushing love away again because I was scared.

But deep down, I knew I had a choice to make: keep our friendship safe, or risk it for the most effortless, exciting love I'd ever felt.

Because with him? There was no performance required. He knew me—my fears, my moods, my walls. He didn't need an explanation; he just got it. Being around him felt like exhaling after holding my breath for years. It was like finally laying down on something soft after running barefoot on concrete. It wasn't loud or dramatic. It was present. Easy. Safe.

And that kind of love? It's rare. Dangerous in its own way because you don't stumble across it often. When you do, it feels like home—not the chaotic kind of home you had to survive, but the kind you always imagined existed if someone truly saw you.

With him, it felt like we had already lived a hundred lifetimes side by side. Like this wasn't the beginning—it was the continuation of something written long before. A soul-familiar connection that made me want to believe maybe, just maybe, this time would be different.

But that scared me.

The War Within

Every time someone showed up to really love me, I panicked. Not because I didn't want them, but because I didn't trust myself not to hurt them. My history was heartbreak. My pattern was sabotage. I didn't know how to exist in love without bracing for the fall. The more someone cared, the more I'd pull away—sabotaging before they had the chance to leave. That's what trauma teaches you: *stay ready so you don't have to get ready.*

So there I was, face to face with something beautiful, and I hesitated. Not because he wasn't enough—he was. He loved me from a place of friendship, history, and genuine care. He saw me—not just the strong version I let the world see, but the soft, broken parts too. And he didn't run. I was safe here.

But safety was unfamiliar. And trauma doesn't trust unfamiliar.

I hadn't forgiven myself for the ways I'd mishandled love before—for the people I hurt, the ones I pushed away, the ones I couldn't love back because I was scared to be seen. I didn't trust myself to choose him and protect him. I only knew how to protect myself.

And you see how quickly I made myself the villain? How I immediately assumed I would be the one to ruin it? It never even crossed my mind that he could hurt me, that he could change, that he could stop showing up. I shouldered all the blame before anything even happened, because that's where my bar was for love: *just don't leave me, and I'll carry the rest.*

But love—real love—doesn't work like that. It requires balance, mutual protection, shared responsibility. It can't thrive in fear. It can't grow in the soil of self-doubt.

So, even in this love that felt like home, I was still quietly at war with myself. Wanting to dive in, terrified I'd drown.

Here's what I'm learning: fear doesn't mean it isn't right. Fear means it's real. Fear means you care. And sometimes the most radical, healing thing you can do when you stumble across a love that feels safe… is to stay soft enough to receive it.

A New Relationship

So we vibing. Things are good—like really good. He feels like an answered prayer. We haven't posted each other or done the whole "this my man" social media thing. It's just been us, enjoying each other. He's been staying over. Collin loves him. And most importantly, he helped me out of a really dark place. My peace was returning. I was grounded. Life was finally smooth.

But of course, when it's too smooth, something always comes to shake the table.

One night, he gets a call. His baby mother is outside of my damn house.

Me? I'm not even confrontational. I don't raise my voice, don't get into screaming matches. I don't do ghetto drama. But here we are. He goes outside to deal with it. I hear her getting loud. So now I gotta go outside too. I'm irritated—why are you here?

She hits me with the classic line: "He said it wasn't nothing, and now y'all together?"

And I'm like, "Girl… your y'all problem has nothing to do with me. Don't bring that energy to my doorstep."

We went back and forth. I tried to keep cool. She was amped. But what pissed me off the most? She hinted that they were still intimate. At this point, I'm livid—but I'm also like, we're not even officially together. Fix your mess.

She kept popping up. Even got disrespectful at their son's game. And that time? I matched her energy. We were out in public, going at it. And I couldn't believe it—I was now beefing with a woman who shouldn't even know my name. She was nowhere near on my level, and yet, here we were. It felt humiliating.

Eventually, he got everything under control, and I didn't have to deal with her again. But I noticed something shifted—he stopped talking about her. Like completely. No updates, no transparency. Just silence. I let it slide because everything else was good.

But the deeper we got, the more I noticed things missing.

See, I had become accustomed to affection—to romance. My old head spoiled me with flowers, gifts, the little things that said *"you matter."* And in this relationship? It felt like that spark, that romantic touch, wasn't there. We were best friends. He helped, held his weight, showed up for me… but I wasn't getting the softness I craved. I needed words of affirmation, emotional connection, gestures that said *I see you.* But instead, I felt like I was hugging a wall—present but not emotionally open.

So, I started to pull back. I matched his energy. But the thing is—when I pull back, it's felt. Loudly. And that's when he admitted something that cut deep.

He said loving me made him feel like he was losing himself.

He felt how I used to feel in relationships—like he was doing so much that he couldn't breathe. He even said he felt like my errand boy. That stung. Especially because I've been that girl in the past with men I didn't respect, but not him. I held him in the highest regard. I thought we were building.

But that was his perception. And perception is reality.

I explained how his withdrawal felt like abandonment to me. And once I feel that, I emotionally flee. You say you want space? I'm moving to Hong Kong. I warned him that I don't come back the same. Each time we disconnect, I love less. I give less. Until there's nothing left.

We talked. Somehow we reconciled. I can't even remember the details—it's a blur. But the impact stuck.

Then it happened again.

And this time, the message was clear: *I'm too much.*

That hit a nerve. A deep one. It mirrored everything I felt during the Home Base situation. My brain didn't know the difference—it registered this as the same trauma. I cried as if I was being left all over again. And maybe I was. Not by him—but by the version of me that still thought love would save her.

I tried to stay. I tried to soften. But I was triggered. And when I'm triggered, I shut down. Not out of spite—but out of survival.

Because deep down, I still believed love had to hurt to be real. And the second I felt that sting, I assumed I had to run.

But he was able to provide reassurance, and just like that, we got back to it. Things smoothed over, but I'd be lying if I said I wasn't wary. He had planted a seed of doubt, and now I wasn't sure if he was truly capable of loving me the way I needed to be loved. What I was asking for didn't feel like too much. It was basic—to be affirmed, prioritized, poured into. He knew what it took to love me. He came after me. He studied me. He knew the role and made it seem like he was built for it. And now he's saying it's moving too fast? That he didn't give himself enough time?

That confused me.

But then came the follow-up: *"I love you. I want this. I just got scared."* He said he realized what he had and didn't want to lose it. That this was the best love he'd ever known. And honestly, I felt the same. We had something rare, and we both knew if we didn't make it work, we'd lose our friendship too. So, we made an understanding. We agreed to show up differently.

But it happened again.

This time, we didn't talk for almost a month. I did what I always do when someone goes ghost—I tried to move on. I entertained other people, tried to distract myself. But then, like clockwork, came the text. The regrets. The *"can we talk?"* And we met up at Outback.

That dinner was the moment I betrayed myself.

I walked into that restaurant knowing what I needed to do. I knew this man wasn't ready. I knew he needed time. I knew he would eventually hurt me—not on purpose, but out of self-preservation. He'd already told me he felt like he was losing himself, and I know what happens when people feel that way. They start to choose themselves. They shut down, pull back, retreat—and I didn't know what version of him would show up when that kicked in. I also didn't want to ruin the friendship we had. That dinner was the perfect exit point.

But I didn't take it.

He said all the right things. That this is what he wanted. That he was going to do what it takes. That he was just in his head, but now he was ready to step into *"us."* And I believed him. I chose to believe him. And in doing so, I walked back into the same storm, telling myself it was a sunny day.

Moving In

Then came the catalyst. My lease was up. I needed to move. My credit was shot and I was facing a $10K move-in cost. I had a friend willing to put a place in his name for me, but Best offered something else—he told me to move in with him. He wanted me to save money, get on my feet. He said he could use the help, too.

I was scared. Terrified, actually. I had never lived with a man before —not with my child. My ex moved in with me that was a little different. That was me entering his space. I had always kept my son separate from my situations. But this time? I trusted him. I believed in the vision. I put all my eggs in that basket. My ancestors told me better. I felt them whispering. But I did it anyway. I moved in.

And that decision? It changed everything.

When I sit and really reflect, I realize there wasn't always a real issue—but there was always something. Some kind of conflict. Most of the time, it was over dumb, petty stuff, and I started to feel like we were in a constant power struggle. Like nobody wanted to say they were wrong first. It wasn't always loud, either. Sometimes it showed up in the smallest ways—little comments, microaggressions that let me know something was off. That's how I knew there was a problem. He wouldn't come out and say it; he'd just throw shade in the form of jokes or passive remarks.

And that was crazy because, in every other area of his life, he was great at communication. But with me? It was like his mouth only worked after I brought up my issue. That used to set me off. Because now we're not even dealing with what I said—now you're bringing up your own issue in response, like tit for tat. And at that point? Your issue feels invalid. I'm already hot. It feels like deflection. It feels like you're not hearing me—just waiting for your turn to speak.

We would go days without talking, just cold energy, side-eyes, and silence. It turned into attitude wars—who could care less, who could stay quiet longer. And I don't do that. I used to stress the importance of communication because silence triggers me. If you go distant for no reason, I will emotionally detach. I've learned how to cut feelings off as protection, and that's not healthy—but it's real.

He'd also make jokes that rubbed me the wrong way. Comments about how I spend money—calling me a drug dealer because I could afford nice dinners and spoil myself. But those jokes didn't feel like jokes. They felt like subtle digs. Like low-key resentment dressed up as humor. And I didn't like it. Because if I've worked hard to create a life where I can enjoy Chilean seabass and oysters on a random Wednesday, I deserve to do that without being mocked. It was giving insecure.

That relationship taught me to start listening with more than my ears. I began paying attention to what wasn't being said—the energy shifts, the tone, the facial expressions. When you constantly have to guess how someone feels, you're not in a relationship — you're in a mind game. That guessing keeps you in your head, second-guessing everything you say and do. And that kind of emotional uncertainty can mess with your peace and your confidence. You start overanalyzing texts, reading between the lines, trying to decode silence or mixed signals. It's exhausting, and worse — it can start making you feel like you're the problem when really, the issue is that they're not communicating.

Plus, when someone doesn't express how they feel or keeps you in the dark, it often means they benefit from your confusion. They keep the power while you're left chasing clarity. That dynamic can easily become manipulative—even if it's not intentional. Real love doesn't keep you guessing. Real love lets you know.

This was something I had dealt with before—with Home Base. That push-pull, keep-you-off-balance dynamic. And I told myself I wasn't about to get manipulated again. So what happened? I got hypervigilant. I started over-analyzing, looking between the lines for ulterior motives. My body remembered betrayal, and my brain went on alert.

Suddenly, where I used to rub his head and be all affectionate, I found myself pulling back. I used to get excited when he came around. I was Tanisha—soft, present, nurturing. He loved that version of me. But once I wasn't sure what energy he was on, Shantrece had to step in. That's the thing about trauma—it doesn't always show up as fear. Sometimes it shows up as armor.

Now I wasn't loving freely. I was loving in response to my environment. Everything became reactionary. He wasn't being affectionate?

Then neither was I. But while he may have just been going through something, I was building resentment. I started to notice the things he used to do were fading—like taking Collin to practice. I was over-whelmed, stressed, and in a relationship that suddenly didn't feel supportive. And that yearning started creeping in—that feeling like I needed more.

Now, historically, this would be the point where I'd level the playing field. Add an extra contestant. Distract myself with something shiny and new. But this time was different. I had grown. So instead of detaching, I told him: I'm not happy.

That was new for me—speaking up. Usually, I'd just leave or cheat. But not this time. I practiced what I wanted to say, nervous because the last thing I ever want to do is make someone feel like they're not enough. But I couldn't keep quiet. I was different now. I had changed.

And to my surprise, the conversation went well. He received it. He acknowledged that he hadn't been showing up the way he needed to. He was struggling—feeling down, depressed, like he wasn't enough. And that, I could understand. What hurt was that he didn't tell me. I'm your partner—you're supposed to lean on me.

I told him how smart he was, how much I trusted him, and how much I believed in him. I reminded him that he wasn't in it alone. Just like he showed up for me, I was ready to show up for him. We made a plan. I'd help more financially, help get a second car, and do what I could to take some of the weight off his shoulders.

A few weeks later, he sent me a message saying how glad he was that we talked, how much lighter he felt. That meant everything to me. I was still uneasy, still wrestling with my own fears—but I chose to stay. I chose softness. I chose us.

Because this time, he wasn't abandoning me. He was just going through something. And I was trying—to love, to grow, to soothe myself through the discomfort, and to remain open in a time where he needed me most. And finally, just like that, we started getting things in motion again. Together. We were doing well—or at least I thought we were. The car plan had gone smoothly, and I'd promised to take the kids to SkyZone. Best stayed behind. I was a little annoyed he didn't come with us, but I told myself he was tired. Cool. I let it go.

But the kids forgot something, so we had to turn back. That's when everything changed. As I pulled into the driveway, I saw him in the car. Immediately, I was irritated—I thought you were tired? But it was what happened next that sent fire through my body.

As I got closer, my car's Bluetooth hijacked my music. A woman's voice came through loud and clear: "Baby, look at my sausage…" I froze. My chest tightened. That voice wasn't mine. His phone had connected to my car. Caller ID lit up—AP. I stepped out, calm but burning inside. "Aye, Yo who you on the phone with?" I asked, trying to give him one last chance to be real.

He fumbled. "My homegirl," he said. And that was it. I didn't argue. I didn't flip out. I took the kids to SkyZone like I promised. And he didn't call, didn't text, didn't try to explain. Some would call that disrespect. But to me? That was respect for my intelligence. He knew not to come at me with no bullshit.

We didn't speak the rest of the day. Later that night—around 3 AM—he finally confessed. He'd been talking to a girl on and off. Wow. So while I was trying to fix things, trying to hold space for him through his "depression," he had someone else calling him "baby." A whole girl comfortable enough to say that, knowing he lived with me.

Karma? Maybe. But it cut deep. He knew my history. He knew the betrayal I had survived, and still chose to do it to me. That's what stung the most. I never did that to him. I respected him. I protected him. But he couldn't offer me the same in return.

And when I asked why—he had nothing. No excuse. He wasn't lonely. I cooked. I showed up. I never told him no. I thought we were good. And yet, the one time I chose not to cheat, I got cheated on. Again.

I never saw it coming. I thought if we didn't work, it would be over a power struggle, not this. Not infidelity. What made it worse? I knew I should've left back at Outback. I knew he wasn't ready. But I stayed. I chose to believe him. And his excuse? That he was going to break up with me anyway. That he felt like he was losing himself. That he hadn't taken time for himself after his last relationship. That he fell out of love with me.

Those words hit like a ton of bricks. And just like that, I couldn't breathe. Again. But this time, I knew what to do. I stopped and sat with the pain. I asked myself the questions I always try to avoid:

- What am I feeling?
- What am I thinking?
- What is my perspective?

And you know what kept coming up? Me ignoring me!

I had to ask: Why did I let my heart override the facts? Was it because I needed to believe it would work? Or was it the people-pleaser in me—afraid to hurt him, even if it meant hurting me?

I Broke the Cycle

I did it again. I failed to keep Tanisha safe. I ignored her gut, silenced her voice, and let her carry the weight of a love that was never meant for her. I knew better—and still, I hoped harder. I gave the benefit of the doubt, bent the truth in his favor, and betrayed my own. I couldn't even stomach being near him as he was evidence of my latest betrayal against me. My thoughts attacked him but in the end what happened is what I thought was going to happen.

What happened is what happens when we ignore our core needs. According to Brianna Wiest in *The Mountain Is You*, when we ignore our core needs, we don't just neglect ourselves—we begin to self-destruct. She explains that self-sabotage is often not laziness, but unmet needs playing out in disguise. It's your subconscious screaming for attention in ways that aren't always healthy. His unmet need was taking time for himself and focusing on self. But he wanted this relationship so he wanted to move forward despite taking that time. But he needed so he took it while being with me. He was attempting to choose me over himself and his survival skills wouldn't let him. I knew that and still let him convince me he could override science and his own innate needs.

When your core needs—things like love, safety, stability, connection, or purpose—are ignored long enough, your mind and body will find a way to get your attention. That's when you start procrastinating, picking the wrong partners, staying stuck in cycles, or settling for less. You're not broken—you're misaligned. You're acting out what you haven't healed.

Wiest says it clearly: when we fail to meet our needs in conscious ways, we'll meet them in unconscious, often destructive ways. So ignoring your needs doesn't make them go away—it just forces them to show up as sabotage, burnout, anxiety, addiction, or toxic patterns in relationships.

To climb your personal "mountain," you have to get honest about what you need, and then make it your responsibility to give it to yourself. He wasn't honest about what he needed and I ended up paying for it.

And now? Guess who's here.

Shantrece.

And thank God.

Not a second too late.

She's not here to rage or break things—she's here to protect. To reclaim. To remind me that every time I ignore my intuition, I pay the price. And this time? That price was me. But no more.

Because now, the boundaries are up. The lesson has landed. The pattern is clear. And I'm finally done playing myself.

Let Shantrece handle it.

I love when she shows up. Shantrece don't do all that crying and spiraling—she's cold, calculated, and logical. She's the one who finishes degrees, lands jobs, makes big moves with no hand-holding. She was killing shit out in D.C. Tanisha? She just wants love. A family. Softness. She's the one who still believes in happily ever after. The career? The accolades? She could take it or leave it.

But not Shantrece. So the game was back on.

Relationship over. Back to regularly scheduled programming. I shifted gears fast—found an apartment, submitted the application, and was ready to be gone in under 30 days. No crying, no second-guessing, just execution.

But before I could even get out... Best had a revelation. A come-to-Jesus moment.

Suddenly, he realized his mistake. He wanted me to come back. Come back?

Oh, so now you see it?

This is what we talked about. The push and pull. The pattern. And just like that—he tried to suck me back into it. But the difference now? I saw it. I named it. I understood it.

And I refused to stay stuck in it. I broke the cycle. I can't betray me again for him. He wants me to. He has done all the things I have asked. It is even better than before. But this is my pattern I ignore past behaviors when someone is nice to me again. I will get mad but I don't stay mad. Its like I get mad.. Get numb and then its like it never happened. I have to change that. He is determined to win me back but who is he looking for Tanisha… My trauma never wants to be soft again… it's not safe.

* * *

TRENCH LESSON

Lesson Learned:

Familiarity isn't always love—it can be trauma in disguise. Real love feels like safety, not chaos. And the first step to finding "the one" is becoming the one for yourself.

Reflection Questions:

- Do I confuse emotional intensity with real connection?
- Where have I abandoned myself in relationships while waiting to be chosen?
- What does safety in love look like to me—and how can I practice giving that to myself first?

Survival Strategy:

Date yourself. Pour into you before pouring into anyone else. Build love maps with yourself—your needs, your boundaries, your joy. That way, when someone shows up, you'll know if they align with the peace you've already created.

Affirmation:

"I am worthy of love that feels safe, steady, and true. I choose me first, so I never abandon myself for love again."

Your Reflection:

Alright, it's your turn. Use the space below to respond to the Trench Lesson activity and be real with yourself—no filters, no judgment.

_____

_____

_____

_____

_____

_____

_____

_____

_____

_____

_____

_____

_____

_____

_____

_____

_____

_____

_____

_____

_____

_____

_____

_____

_____

_____

_____

_____

_____

_____

CHAPTER 13
WHERE AM I NOW

This process isn't linear; healing never is. Some days you wake up like the war is over, filled with peace, finally breathing easy. Other days, you're right back in the trenches, wrestling with old wounds in a new body, dodging bullets that look like memories.

But what I know now is this: you have to choose you, even when it hurts. Even when it disappoints others. You have to put logic over emotion, clarity over chaos. And to do that, you need your armor. Not the heavy, suffocating armor of Shantrece. She is a trauma response, a built persona for safety. I created her a long time ago; I just finally understand my parts and their purpose. We all have a Shantrece. While she is effective on the battlefield, she is also detrimental to love. Shantrece is not intimacy—she is defense. A set of weapons and shields designed to dismantle whatever looks like a threat, even when that "threat" is someone trying to love us.

Now today, love is seen as a threat to our lives. The brain processes emotional pain the same way it does physical pain. When you get your heart broken, the same parts of your brain light up as if you were physically hurt—like the anterior cingulate cortex and the insula, the same places that activate when you break a bone or get burned. That's why it hits so hard. Your body doesn't know the difference. So when I was laid out over these men, it wasn't just drama—it was my nervous system going into shock. The brain literally can't tell the difference between a breakup and a wound, so it treats them the same.

That's why the tears don't feel like enough. That's why your chest hurts. That's why heartbreak will have you thinking you're about to die—because in a way, something inside you did.

And if that happens every time you love—if every connection ends with your chest caving in and your world flipped upside down—what do you think your brain is going to start associating with love? Danger. Pain. Threat. That's when the wiring gets messed up. Your nervous system stops seeing love as something warm and safe, and starts preparing for war every time it shows up.

So even when something good comes along, your body's already in defense mode. That's why we self-sabotage. That's why we shut down or cling too hard. That's why healthy love feels foreign. Because to your brain, love equals hurt. And the scary part? It starts to expect it. Now love has to fight through all your trauma just to land.

Many of us don't want to fight anymore—we're tired. We've loved hard, fallen harder, and been left picking up the pieces alone. So we gave up. Not just on people, but on love itself. We tell ourselves we're better off numb. We bury our softness under sarcasm, sex, silence, and self-preservation. And honestly? I get it. Because when heartbreak starts to feel inevitable, surrender feels like protection.

But what happens to a world where everyone gives up?

We're already seeing it. It's in our families—where people don't talk, just tolerate. It's in our communities—where trust is scarce and connection feels dangerous. It's in our dating culture—where passion is replaced with power plays and people collect bodies instead of building bonds.

A quiet war is unfolding, and no one's really winning. Because the world isn't just tired—it's suffering from Relationship Traumatic Stress Syndrome (RTSS).

We've normalized dysfunction so long we mistake it for compatibility. We bond through trauma, ghost to protect ourselves, and confuse chaos with chemistry. And while we're busy trying not to get hurt, love is bleeding out. Slowly. Quietly. Tragically.

RTSS isn't just a personal problem. It's a cultural epidemic. And if we don't start healing it—collectively—we will raise another generation who doesn't know how to love or be loved.

So no, this isn't just about your ex. This is about saving the future of love.

Time to suit up. Sorry, I got a little carried away. I don't want you to try and fight the war, but examine yourself and how you show up in relationships. Do your part and heal. Get help and start to ask yourself some questions.

Ask yourself: are you the issue? Do you have a problem where peace feels foreign and chaos feels like home? Do you find yourself in the same arguments, with different people, over and over? Do your relationships become a mirror—reflecting back your unhealed wounds instead of your worth?

It's not just about the people you're choosing; it's about the patterns you're repeating.

Acknowledging that means being brutally honest with yourself. Not just about what they did—but about what you did. The thoughts you kept quiet. The feelings you ignored. The red flags you romanticized. The moments when you needed love but chose performance. When you abandoned your own needs to avoid being abandoned.

That's where the healing begins: when you can sit with your own discomfort and trace it back—not to blame, but to understand.

Are you afraid? Of course you are. We all are. Afraid to be alone. Afraid to be hurt again. Afraid that we are too broken to be loved in the way we need. But ask yourself—are you staying in survival mode because it's safer than vulnerability? Are you avoiding love because you think it will destroy you?

Now ask something even harder: do any of your relationships look like mine? Or maybe, just maybe, do you act like one of my partners?

Emotionally unavailable, hyper-independent, cold, controlling, avoidant, inconsistent, passive-aggressive, manipulative—but charming. Loving but not loving well.

You've read these pages. Maybe cried. Maybe laughed. Maybe got defensive as hell. Maybe saw yourself in too many of these stories. And now you're sitting there like—damn... this is me.

Good. That means you're awake now.

You don't heal by hiding. You don't grow by pretending you got it all figured out. The moment you said "this is me," you stopped lying to yourself. And that's where the real shit starts.

Here's what you do now:

Before you can heal, you have to stop running. Sit with the ache. Let it sting. Let it settle in your bones and teach you something. Don't numb it with distractions or go looking for someone new to help you forget. Instead, ask the hard questions: *When did I learn to love like this? Why do I choose people who can't choose me back? When did I stop choosing myself?* That's where your work begins.

But be gentle with yourself, too. You're not broken. You're not beyond repair. You did what you had to do with the tools you had. Survival got you here, but it won't get you free. Healing requires softness. It asks for truth. It demands that you love yourself in ways you never learned growing up. That kind of love starts with grace.

Ask for help. Talk to someone. Get in therapy. Scream into a pillow if you need to—but stop pretending you have to carry it all on your own. You've been strong long enough. Let someone teach you a new way to be.

And don't rush back into dating. Don't try to get over someone by getting under someone else. Be still. Let your nervous system breathe. Figure out who you are when no one is texting you back. Learn what peace feels like so you stop mistaking chaos for chemistry.

Then, check your patterns. Don't just ask why they hurt you—ask why you stayed. Why you ignored the red flags. Why you kept performing for love instead of asking for what you needed. These are the questions that will save your life.

And even when it's boring, even when nobody's watching—keep showing up for you. Healing isn't glamorous. It's boundaries. It's silence. It's drinking water, deleting numbers, crying in the shower, and still getting up for work. But every baby step counts.

Most of all, choose yourself. Every single day. Not in a trendy, surface-level way, but in the real way—saying no when it's easier to say yes. Walking away even when you still love them. Being done even when you're still tempted. That's what loving yourself really looks like.

Healing from Trauma

Step 1: Understand the Trauma Loop
(TF-CBT Framework)

You are not just reacting to a person. You are reacting to a pattern. Trauma-Focused Cognitive Behavioral Therapy (TF-CBT) explains that emotional wounds exist within *loops*—cycles of thoughts, feelings, and behaviors triggered by past pain. Until you identify and break that loop, you'll continue reliving the same relationship stories in new bodies.

Example Trauma Loop:

- *Trigger:* They ignore your message.
- *Thought*: "I'm not important."
- *Feeling:* Shame, fear, panic
- *Behavior:* Over-texting, emotional shutdown, self-blame

Journal Prompts:

- What patterns have you noticed in your relationships?
- What thoughts surface when you feel ignored, unloved, or unseen?
- What younger version of you is being activated?

The goal isn't blame—it's awareness. Because what you don't name, you will unknowingly repeat.

Step 2: Confront Your Need for External Validation
(Self-Worth Theory + Inner Child Work)

If you need someone to love you to feel okay, you will always be vulnerable to destruction in their absence.

Many of us were raised to earn affection. We internalized that love is conditional, and now we chase validation as proof of our worth. But validation is not the same as value.

To reclaim your self-worth:

- Detach your identity from your relationship status.
- Separate rejection from your value.
- Learn to see yourself through your own compassionate gaze.

Ask yourself: *Who am I without their affirmation?* If that question feels hollow, that's the wound.ou are not needy. You are healing from a life of unmet needs. Your job is to become the one who validates you first.

Step 3: Learn and Shift Your Attachment Style
(Attachment Theory)

You are not doomed by your attachment style. You can earn security.

Attachment theory reveals that we love according to what we learned. Anxious, avoidant, and disorganized patterns are survival responses—not character flaws.

Securely attached people:

- Communicate needs without guilt
- Regulate emotions without blame
- Trust others without losing themselves
- Feel safe, even in discomfort

To begin shifting toward secure attachment:

- *Co-regulate:* Surround yourself with relationships that model safety and consistency. You must participate in relationships that will create experiences that contradict negative core beliefs.

- *Self-soothe:* Calm your body without external approval. This is important as you have to know how to calm yourself.

- *Set boundaries:* Say no without guilt, and yes without fear of losing control.

- *Repair:* Name ruptures and repair instead of withdrawing or escalating.

Healing isn't the absence of fear; it's the presence of safety even when fear arises.

Step 4: Regulate Instead of React
(TF-CBT + Somatic Healing)

The body remembers what the mind tries to forget. You're not just thinking your way into panic, you're *feeling* your way there. If your nervous system has been wired for abandonment, even stable love can feel threatening.

You must teach your body that safety doesn't mean shutdown. When triggered, try replacing reactions with regulation.

Instead of:

- Texting in desperation
- Stalking their social media
- Replaying old conversations

Try:

- Grounding techniques (5-4-3-2-1 method)
- Somatic movement (shaking, tapping, stretching)
- Breathwork or prayer
- Journaling from your inner child's voice

You're not just calming yourself. You're training your body to trust that peace is possible.

Step 5: Rewrite Your Belief System
(CBT + Narrative Therapy)

Breakups don't just end relationships, they often confirm old stories.

- "I'm not enough."
- "No one stays."
- "I always get left."

These beliefs are not facts; they are fossils from childhood. They're the stories you told yourself when your emotional needs weren't met.

To reconstruct your narrative:

- Identify the belief
- Ask, "Whose voice is this?"
- Ask, "How old was I when I started believing this?"
- Challenge the thought with evidence that contradicts negative thoughts and gives compassion

Self-worth isn't built from mantras alone. It's built from stacking new experiences that contradict the old ones.

Step 6: Create Safety with Boundaries
(Relational Ethics)

Boundaries are how you teach people how to love you *without losing yourself.* They are not walls, they are doors with locks that *you* control.

Post-breakup boundaries might look like:

- Enforcing no contact (temporarily or permanently)
- Avoiding mutual spaces or conversations about them
- Saying no to friends who minimize your pain
- Protecting your peace even when it disappoints others

As a recovering people-pleaser, you may have built your life around others' feelings. But empathy without boundaries becomes self-betrayal. Boundaries are how you say: "I will not abandon myself again."

Step 7: Practice Self-Compassion and Forgiveness
(Self-Compassion Theory)

Forgiveness isn't about excusing what happened—it's about releasing yourself from the identity that trauma created.

Forgive yourself for:

- Believing they were your forever
- Tolerating more than you should've
- Betraying your intuition
- Abandoning yourself to keep the peace

Speak to yourself the way you needed to be spoken to when you were hurting the most. Apologize to you. Validate you. Hold space for you.

Healing is not linear. Some days you will miss them. Some days you'll want to reach out. That doesn't mean you've failed—it means you're still human. Just come back to yourself.

Step 8: Envision and Build the Life You Want to Come Home To
(Post-Traumatic Growth + Joe Dispenza's Visualization Work)

You don't just heal by letting go. You heal by building something new.

Joe Dispenza teaches that if you want to change your life, you must first change your *identity*. You must rehearse your future so vividly that your body begins to believe it now.

Ask yourself:

- Who are you when you're no longer surviving?
- What does your morning routine look like?
- How do you talk to yourself?
- What kind of people do you attract?
- What standards do you no longer negotiate?

Practice:

- Design a "day in the life" of your healed self.
- Meditate daily from the *end result*—as if it's already yours.
- Visualize your nervous system calm, your heart open, your self-worth untouchable.

Don't wait for peace to come through another person.
Become the peace.

Don't wait for the apology.
Become the closure.

Don't wait for someone to choose you.
Choose yourself—so loudly that no one else's rejection can ever silence you again.

Final Note:

You are not healing to be chosen. You are healing so you never again abandon *yourself* in the name of love. You already did the hardest part. You told the truth. Now let's see what happens when *you stop abandoning yourself.*

* * *

TRENCH LESSON

Lesson Learned:

Healing means choosing yourself, even when it feels uncomfortable, even when it costs you people you thought you couldn't live without. Survival mode might have kept you alive, but it will never let you thrive.

Reflection Questions:

- Where have I been settling for chaos because peace feels unfamiliar?
- Do my relationships reflect my worth—or my wounds?
- When was the last time I abandoned myself to keep someone else?

Survival Strategy:

Trade the armor for awareness. Shantrece may have kept you safe, but she's not built for love. Start noticing when you go into defense mode —when you shut down, joke away the pain, or chase validation. Pause. Breathe. Choose softness over survival. Seek therapy, accountability, and real connection.

Affirmation:

"I am no longer at war with myself. I choose peace. I choose clarity. I choose me—every time."

Your Reflection:

Alright, it's your turn. Use the space below to respond to the Trench Lesson activity and be real with yourself—no filters, no judgment.

_____

_____

_____

_____

_____

_____

_____

_____

_____

_____

_____

_____

_____

_____

_____

_____

_____

_____

_____

_____

_____

_____

_____

_____

_____

_____

_____

_____

_____

CHAPTER 14
SOME SHIT YOU SHOULD KNOW...

I n this final section, I share answers to three frequently asked questions. Think of it as a cheat sheet for your healing journey— straight talk, no fluff. These are the things I wish someone had told me sooner, the things that might save you from circling the same cycles I did.

* * *

1. How do you love safely?

You love safely when you stop making pain a requirement. For years, I thought love had to be complicated. That if it didn't hurt a little, it wasn't real. I confused anxiety for butterflies, silence for mystery, and inconsistency for passion. But that wasn't love—that was my trauma trying to be seen.

Loving safely means choosing peace over performance. It means honoring your boundaries, even when someone tries to make you feel guilty for having them. It's knowing that the moment you start begging for clarity, you've already lost yourself.

I had to ask myself: Am I actually attracted to this person, or am I addicted to proving I'm worthy of being chosen?

Reading *Attached* by Amir Levine cracked me wide open. I wasn't "needy"—I had an anxious attachment style. My nervous system was wired to crave reassurance, not chaos. Now? I don't chase. I choose. If it's not consistent, calm, and clear, I don't want it. I don't argue with red flags anymore—I honor them. No long texts. No tears. Just boundaries and a soft exit.

2. How do you identify a healthy relationship?

A healthy relationship feels like safety. It's not performative. It's not perfect. It's peaceful. Think: mutual respect, emotional responsiveness, shared values, and honest communication. According to the Gottman Institute, the strongest relationships have more bids than battles—moments where you turn toward each other instead of away.

A good partner doesn't just tell you they love you—they show up when it matters. They validate your feelings, not gaslight them. They support your healing, not weaponize your past. And they're consistent —not just when it's convenient, but when it's hard.

3. What are the red flags to let you know when it's time to disconnect?

If you're always confused, it's not love—it's manipulation. Red flags aren't always loud. Sometimes they're quiet: emotional unavailability, avoidance, weaponized silence, jokes that sting, delayed responses, or always needing to "think" about the relationship.

If they make you doubt yourself more than they make you feel seen, you're in danger. Amy Chan said it best in *Breakup Bootcamp*— "Your relationship is either a lesson or a mirror." If it's teaching you pain on repeat, it's time to walk. The longer you stay, the harder it is to leave.

When your nervous system is finally calm around someone—that's your body saying, this is safe. And that's the love you deserve.

No more chaos. No more guessing. Just clarity. Peace. Softness. That's the new standard. *Okay, I'm done...*

* * *

If you take nothing else from this, take this: loving safely starts with loving yourself safely first. That means setting boundaries and not abandoning yourself just to keep someone else around. It means recognizing that healthy relationships feel calm, not chaotic. They don't make you question your worth, or force you to beg for the basics. A good partner shows up—consistently, respectfully, and with intention.

We now know that love without boundaries isn't love—it's self-betrayal. Those anxious spirals? They aren't love, they're trauma responses. And those red flags we kept ignoring? They were never going to turn green. The truth is: familiarity isn't always safety. Sometimes it's just a loop we haven't learned how to break.

You want to know when to disconnect? When you keep shrinking. When you start compromising your peace, your voice, your joy just to maintain the connection. When your nervous system is always in defense mode. When you forget who you are trying to prove you're worthy of love. That's when it's time to go.

This journey—this healing—it's not cute. It's not easy. But it's necessary. Because we can't keep calling pain love and expecting different results. We can't keep showing up wounded and wondering why we're bleeding all over people who didn't cut us.

So, suit up. Heal for real. Love, but love wisely. And whatever you do—don't lose yourself again.

You deserve love that's safe, honest, mutual, and freeing. Anything less isn't love—it's a lesson. And baby, we've had enough lessons. It's time to graduate.

By the way...

If you made it this far, thank you. But more importantly—please read. Like really read. Go back and reread the things that made you pause, the parts that stung, the lines that felt too real. Because reading is fundamental, and it just might save your life the way it started to save mine.

Reading gave me language for things I thought were just personal flaws. It showed me I wasn't crazy, I was triggered. I wasn't broken, I was wounded. It helped me normalize my patterns, trace my behaviors, and start telling the truth—to myself first. That insight? That awareness? That's where the healing begins.

So, pick up *Attached*. Flip through *Breakup Bootcamp*. Study the Gottman principles. Don't just read to feel seen—read to get free. You're not alone. You're not hopeless. You just have to start doing the work—and baby, if you're reading this, you already have. Keep going. This isn't the end. It's the beginning of your comeback.

* * *

TRENCH LESSON

Lesson Learned:

Safe love doesn't come from chaos—it comes from clarity, peace, and boundaries. Loving safely means choosing consistency over confusion, respect over red flags, and self-trust over self-betrayal.

Reflection Questions:

- Do I mistake anxiety or intensity for love?
- Where have I ignored red flags and called it "chemistry"?
- How can I start practicing loving myself safely so I can recognize safe love when it shows up?

Survival Strategy:

Stop calling pain passion. When the old pull toward chaos rises, pause. Breathe. Ask: *Is this love, or is this my trauma trying to feel familiar?* Build safety inside yourself first—through self-care, prayer, journaling, therapy, and boundaries—so you won't tolerate what undermines your peace.

Affirmation:

"I choose peace over performance, clarity over confusion, and boundaries over self-betrayal. I am worthy of a love that is safe, consistent, and real."

Your Reflection:

Alright, it's your turn. Use the space below to respond to the Trench Lesson activity and be real with yourself—no filters, no judgment.

_____

_____

_____

_____

_____

_____

_____

_____

_____

_____

_____

_____

_____

_____

_____

_____

_____

_____

_____

_____

_____

_____

_____

_____

_____

_____

_____

_____

_____

_____

ACKNOWLEDGMENTS

This book is more than pages; it's the story of my survival, my scars, and my healing. And none of it happened in isolation. I came from a home marked by addiction and chaos, yet God moved mountains to make sure I received the love, guidance, and covering I needed. Where there were gaps, He placed people. Where there was lack, He poured abundance.

To my siblings: there is no one who could ever cover for you or replace you. **Crystal**, my oldest sister, you had to be a mom before your time. Because of you, we are so close. I am thankful for your sacrifices and your love. **Ashley**, my crybaby, I am thankful for your laugh—I don't know what I would do without it. You are the kind one. **Breona**, my mother's twin, there is not a battle you would let me face alone; you would always clear a block for me. **Lor Gregory**, you were supposed to be the last kid. I am so proud of who you have become—my first blood brother! **Brova**, the last one—if it wasn't for me, you would've had a dumb name. I love you. I feel for you because you were robbed. Mommy was taken when you needed her the most, but you have all of us, and we are going to go hard for you! Jasmine, my bonus sister— you stole my mother, but it's okay because you have paid the price to be affiliated. I could always count on you to come running if it's ever a war.

To the women who raised me while my mother fought her battles: **Aunt Neecy**, the first one to take me in—I love you deeply. **Aunt Candy**, you didn't take any mess, and you couldn't tell me I wasn't your child. **Nadia**, you took me under your wing and shaped me into the professional I am today. You made me a director right out of school —you saw things in me that I didn't see in myself.

To my **"Fova"**— you weren't my dad, but you were always a call away. Even in your own storm, you tried to cover me. To my son's godfather, **Khalief** —you were instrumental in helping me understand my worth. You watched me self-destruct and always redirected me with love.

God knew I would struggle with romantic relationships, so He made sure I was rich in friendships. **Booboo**, my first best friend—thank you. When you moved to Pennsylvania, I had the **Mosher Street Girls: Candice, Charmecia, Sharnecia,** and my best friend **Sade**. I remember us going to church all by ourselves—my first friend group. Then Booboo came back—the social one—and with **Amber** and **Patricia**, you showed me how to be a lady, from earrings to lip gloss. Patricia, you hold such a special space in my heart. There's not a thing you let me go through alone. Even when I try to hide, you always know.

God kept pouring. In high school—the toughest years—I had my core group, the **007 Girls: Tierra, Keeyah, Dionne, Lisha,** and **Jazmyne**, who I can still call to this day. Then came my **SAC Girls: Maia, Quita, Brit,** and **Kelz D (RIP)**—my "outside days" when I started hanging out, tightening up, and getting sharper. **Shantrece**—my inner armor—started brewing here.

Throughout my life, there have been so many influential relationships. Even in adulthood, God kept sending people.

To my **Live Benevolent family** and the **Breakfast Club**—there's nothing I can do without y'all. To my brothers from **Winters Lane**, you hold a special place in my heart. No matter what, you gave me a space where I belonged, protected me, and—lowkey—you're the reason I'm spoiled. **Mello**, I can't think of a time you weren't there. No one would dare do anything to me because they didn't want an issue with you. Just like you've always been there for me, I'm here for you until they free you.

Crystal— not only did you raise me before your time, but I owe you for something else too: I stole your friends. All your life you didn't want me hanging with them, and now you're the one telling me to come out. I am so thankful, because I wouldn't have even been on my first trip without them. Through you, I was grandfathered into a group of bosses—the **Edmondson Avenue Girls**—and they welcomed me like family. That sisterhood gave me laughter, support, and memories I'll carry forever.

To **Bae**, thank you for being there through all of this. I know it's not easy—especially seeing me in my "ho-handling" phases and still loving me. You have been here through every chapter. You could've believed the narratives, but you saw who I really am and never left my side. I know I don't make it easy, but thank you for never giving up.

Big Collin, my dog! You gave me my first son— the one who saved me. Our child changed the entire trajectory of my life. We ain't been together in ages, but I know if I need you, there isn't any hesitation. Yes, you will complain, but you are going to come through.

Baby Collin, you are the best thing that has ever happened to me. I go so hard because I want you to have every resource, every opportunity, and every advantage you need for success. More than that, I want you to see me and know that anything is possible—that no matter where you start, you can create the life you deserve. I carry the responsibility of addressing my trauma, not just for me, but for you. So that when you look at me, you don't just see strength—you see healing. So that when you step inside our home, you witness love, safety, and stability. So that you grow up knowing what a healthy relationship looks like and never have to question your worth inside of one.

To every man I encountered— I harbor no hatred for anything you've done. I forgive you. It wasn't you; it was the brokenness in me that allowed me to think what you were giving was love. And I've learned to forgive me, too. To the ones that came with good intentions, I am sorry the broken parts couldn't allow me to see the purity of your intentions. If I caused you any pain, I, too, hope that you can forgive me.

Finally, to **Tanisha Shantrece Williams**— I thank you the most. Thank you for enduring all that you did and still choosing love. Thank you for not letting your story bury you in shame or guilt, but for transforming it into testimony. Thank you for carrying the weight of brokenness, betrayal, and abandonment, and still finding a way to stand tall.

To the little girl inside of me— who once waited by the door for her mother to return, who learned to love people that hurt her, who confused absence for abandonment and chaos for love—I see you now. I know what you needed, and I know what you didn't get. You deserved safety, consistency, joy without strings, and love without conditions. I can't rewrite your childhood, but I can promise you this: as an adult, I will protect you. I will give you the security, tenderness, and nurturing you always longed for. I will not abandon you the way others did. Your needs matter, your voice matters, and I will spend the rest of my life making sure you are safe, seen, and loved.

To the woman I've become— thank you for taking everything life threw at us and turning it into fuel for healing. Thank you for not only surviving, but for creating space where other women can survive and heal too. You turned our trenches into a movement, our heartbreak into a handbook, our wounds into wisdom.

You are proof that survival was never the endgame, healing is.
This book is our survival, our testimony, and our roadmap home.

ABOUT THE AUTHOR

Tanisha Williams was born and raised in Baltimore City, coming from a broken home that taught her both the ache of abandonment and the resilience it takes to survive. She knows what it feels like to confuse chaos with chemistry, to mistake pain for passion, and to lose yourself trying to be chosen. Those early battles left her scarred, but they also gave her a mission.

Tanisha earned her Master's in Marriage, Family, and Couples Counseling and became a Licensed Clinical Professional Counselor because she wanted to turn her pain into purpose. She didn't just study healing in textbooks, she lived it in real time. Today, she helps individuals and families navigate trauma, addiction, and relationships, while continuing to walk her own journey of growth.

She also founded the *HGIC (Healed Gangsta's in Charge) Community*, a movement for women who, like herself, survived the trenches of toxic love and are ready to choose peace over performance, clarity over chaos, and wholeness over wounds.

Tanisha's debut book, *Sh!t I Learned in the Trenches: Love and Trauma — The Survival Guide for Women Who Been Through It*, is both her testimony and a survival guide. It's raw, unfiltered, and rooted in truth, naming the impact of Relationship Traumatic Stress Syndrome (RTSS) while offering tools to finally heal and love safely.

The real flex isn't surviving the trenches.
The real flex is graduating from them.

www.ingramcontent.com/pod-product-compliance
Lightning Source LLC
Chambersburg PA
CBHW051518120626
46551CB00012B/972